Women

Make

The
Difference
Women
Make

*The Policy Impact
of Women in Congress*

Michele L. Swers

The University of Chicago Press
Chicago and London

MICHELE L. SWERS is an assistant professor of government at Georgetown University. She is the winner of the 2001 Carl Albert Award for the best dissertation on legislative politics, presented by the Legislative Studies Section of the American Political Science Association.

The University of Chicago Press, Chicago 60637
The University of Chicago Press, Ltd., London
© 2002 by The University of Chicago
All rights reserved. Published 2002
Printed in the United States of America

11 10 09 08 07 06 05 04 03 02   1 2 3 4 5

ISBN: 0-226-78647-1 (cloth)
ISBN: 0-226-78649-8 (paper)

Library of Congress Cataloging-in-Publication Data

Swers, Michele L.
    The difference women make: the policy impact of women in
Congress / Michele L. Swers
        p. cm.
    Includes bibliographical references and index.
    ISBN 0-226-78647-1 (cloth : alk. paper)—ISBN 0-226-78649-8
(pbk. : alk. paper)
        1. United States. Congress—Voting. 2. Women legislators—
United States. 3. Decision making. 4. United States—Social
policy. 5. United States—Politics and government. I. Title.

JK1051 .S94 2002
320'.6'0973—dc21   2002001060

To my husband,
Andrew Todd Swers

Contents

Tables

Acknowledgments

As a student in high school, I was always drawn to stories about political leaders who overcame the odds and worked to make a difference for the people. After my grandmother, Anne Kurlantzick, gave me a book about Eleanor Roosevelt, I became increasingly interested in the role of women in national politics. A summer course on the subject sealed my interest in the field and planted the seeds for a project about the policy impact of electing women to Congress. I wish to express my gratitude to those who helped me transform this project from an idea into reality.

I am fortunate to have many friends and colleagues who provided intellectual and emotional support throughout the process of writing this book. My thesis advisers at Harvard, Theda Skocpol, Sidney Verba, and John Aldrich, offered guidance and scholarly expertise. Each generously shared their time and research experience, from planning the study design to completion of the project. I would also like to thank Kosuke Imai, Christina Davis, Dan Lipinski, and Karen Rothkin for sharing ideas and commenting on the methodological design. I am grateful to Sue Thomas, Cindy Simon Rosenthal, and Karen O'Connor for commenting on conference papers and introducing me to the women and politics research community. John Tryneski, Anne Ford, Yvonne Zipter, and the anonymous reviewers for the University of Chicago Press helped me to create a better and more readable manuscript. In addition, this project could not be completed without the members of Congress and their staffs, who provided first-hand insights into the congressional policy-making process.

Throughout the writing process, my family, Belle and Theodore Probst, Arlene and Marvin Birnbaum, and Gwen, Ronald, and Jeffrey Swers acted as my personal cheering squad and offered love and support. My grandparents and grandparents-in-law, Anne and David Kurlantzick,

Ruth and Jesse Isaacs, Evelyn and Ralph Herman, and Lillian and Sam Swers, taught me the value of education, hard work, and family.

My deepest thanks go to my husband and best friend, Andrew Swers. As my editor-in-chief, he read every word of every draft. As my computer technician, he insured that I had the latest equipment and fixed every glitch. As my greatest champion and personal knight in shining armor, he believed I could successfully pursue an academic career and made me believe in myself. I dedicate this book to him.

Chapter 1

Does Electing Women Have a Policy Impact?

On October 20, 1999, a group of largely Democratic women took to the floor of the House of Representatives to support an amendment by Congresswoman Patsy Mink (D-HI) that would restore funding for gender equity programs to a Republican bill reauthorizing parts of the 1965 Elementary and Secondary Schools Education Act. As evidence of the continuing need for gender equity programs, Congresswoman Stephanie Tubbs Jones (D-OH) cited women's underrepresentation in Congress. She proclaimed, "Women need to be encouraged to be right here on the floor . . . they need to think about how can we be here on the floor of the U.S. Congress talking about issues that impact the entire country and only fifty-seven of us are women" (*Congressional Record* 1999, October 20, H10502).

Congresswoman Tubbs Jones's comments imply that electing more women to Congress will not just achieve equality but also influence the range of issues considered on the national agenda and the formulation of policy solutions. She is not alone in her belief that electing more women will have a substantive policy impact. Numerous women's Political Action Committees (PACs) raise money to elect liberal or conservative women candidates. For example, the Women in Senate and House (WISH) List raises money for pro-choice Republican women, while the Susan B. Anthony List supports pro-life women (Nelson 1994). In the 2000 election cycle, Early Money Is Like Yeast's (EMILY's) List raised $21,201,339 to support pro-choice, Democratic women, thus making it one of the leading fundraisers among all PACs (Federal Election Commission 2001a, 2001b).[1] Some women candidates even point to their gender as one of the reasons voters should elect them. Announcing her candidacy for the Senate in 1998, Blanche Lambert Lincoln (D-AR) proclaimed that she was running because "nearly one of every three senators is a millionaire, but there are only five mothers" (Greenblatt

1997). Similarly, Patty Murray (D-WA) launched her 1992 Senate campaign as "just a mom in tennis shoes" (Schroedel and Snyder 1994).

Paradoxically, though the level of attention to the potential policy impact of women has increased, one of the more well-established tenets of congressional research asserts that the personal identity of the member is largely irrelevant to the nature of policy outcomes. Congressional scholars maintain that electoral concerns are paramount in the calculus of all representatives (Mayhew 1974; Arnold 1990). Therefore, legislators will respond to the same constituency interests regardless of gender.

How important is it to have a Congress that "looks like America"? Do we need more women as mothers in Congress? Do we need more women as women? This book moves beyond the conventional wisdom concerning the political behavior of women to evaluate whether politically significant social identities such as gender influence the legislative priorities of representatives and under what circumstances these effects occur. To discern the policy impact of electing women, I examine whether congresswomen in the 103rd (1993–94) and 104th (1995–96) Congresses were more likely to support and advocate women's issue legislation than were their male colleagues, once one accounts for the major partisan, ideological, and constituency influences on representatives' policy decisions. Using a specially created database of women's issue bills, I investigate legislators' commitment to women's issues across the legislative process, from the introduction of bills, through committee consideration, to the final roll-call votes. By comparing legislative activity on women's issues in the strikingly different political and institutional climates of the 103rd and 104th Congresses, this research demonstrates how changes in the political context and a member's position within the institution facilitate or constrain a representative's ability to pursue policy preferences based on gender.

Applying Theories of Representation to Women

The political activists, media commentators, and political scientists who call for the election of more women to Congress all share the assumption that electing more women will lead to better representation for women's interests. Hanna Pitkin (1967) describes this relationship as the belief that increasing "descriptive representation" will lead to better "substantive representation." Thus, representatives who share a common social identity, such as gender, race, or class will be more likely to act for the interests of their group (Phillips 1995, 1998; Mansbridge 1999). Additionally, this connection based on shared experiences will improve the deliberative quality of the legislature by allowing for the expression of different perspectives on and solutions to policy problems (Mansbridge 1999).[2]

The concern that Congress does not adequately reflect the breadth of interests in the nation dates back to the founding period. During the debate over the ratification of the Constitution, Anti-Federalists argued that the design of the legislative branch would ensure the election of upper-class men who would not adequately represent the needs of the middling classes of farmers, merchants, and laborers. Thus, in *Letters from the Federal Farmer*, the author proclaims, "If the representation be so formed as to give one or more of the natural classes of men in the society an undue ascendancy over the others, it is imperfect; the former will gradually become masters, and the latter slaves" (Storing 1981, 75). Today the Anti-Federalist concern over the quality of representation provided by Congress is reflected in debates over majority/minority districts, campaign finance reform, and term limits as well as the paucity of women in Congress.

While the *Federal Farmer* highlights the connection between the representative and the interests, needs, and wants of his constituents as the key to the representative relationship, it is not clear that women share distinct interests. As Virginia Sapiro (1981) asked, "On what grounds can we argue that women are entitled to representation as members of a group rather than, simply, as individuals?" Although public attention to the gender gap increased in the 1980s and 1990s, the gender gap is quite small compared to other electoral differences, particularly the race and class gaps (Seltzer, Newman, and Voorhees Leighton 1997). Women do not share a monolithic opinion on all issues, and districts do not incorporate high concentrations of women in the same way that a district might include a majority of blue-collar workers or a large minority population.

Yet evidence from the history of women's political participation, studies of gender-role socialization, and research on women as voters and candidates all demonstrate that women may bring unique experiences and viewpoints to the policy debate and different issues to the legislative agenda. The *Federal Farmer*'s concern for the "natural classes of men" highlights women's history of exclusion from politics. The division of society into public (economic and political) and private (home) spheres formed the basis for this exclusion, and it was assumed that men spoke for themselves and their wives in the area of public affairs (Flexner 1975; Sapiro 1983; Baker 1984). Over time, female political activists worked to eliminate the boundaries between the public and private worlds and to incorporate private-sphere issues into public policy debates. Thus, in the Progressive Era, women justified their entry into policy debates by describing themselves as "civic mothers" who needed to help shape public policy on issues ranging from education to child labor and public sanitation in order to protect their children and families (Baker 1984; Skocpol 1992). In the late 1960s and 1970s, the feminist movement made "the personal political" and focused on gaining economic and social equality for women and attention to women's special needs in such areas as sexual harassment and pregnancy leave (Hartmann 1989; Costain 1992).

Scholars who examine gender-role socialization and its impact on women's attitudes and behavior note that women are raised to accept primary responsibility for the care of young children and elderly relatives. Consequently, women tend to view themselves in relational terms and they focus on contextual factors when seeking solutions to problems while men are raised to differentiate themselves as individuals and to view problems through the lens of abstract rights rather than focusing on the particular circumstances of the situation (e.g., Chodorow 1974; Gilligan 1982; Lips 1995; Flammang 1997; Tong 1998).

Beyond psychological orientation, the emphasis on caregiving has an impact on the social, economic, and political patterns of women's lives. Many women leave the workforce or seek out jobs with flexible schedules in order to take care of young children or elderly relatives. This path allows women more time with their children but also reduces their earning power and can have an impact on their employability as their skills become obsolete (Stetson 1997; Conway, Ahern, and Steuernagel 1999; Costello and Stone 2001).

The need to find employment that will accommodate their family responsibilities, combined with discrimination stemming from the belief that women are not suited to certain jobs, has created a workforce divided by sex. Women are concentrated in low-wage jobs and those that achieve professional success often face a glass ceiling in their efforts to reach the upper echelons of the career ladder. For example, in 1998, women constituted 92.5 percent of registered nurses but only 26.6 percent of physicians, 98.1 percent of dental assistants but only 19.8 percent of dentists, and 84 percent of elementary school teachers but only 42.3 percent of postsecondary educators (Costello and Stone 2001). Race and ethnicity also have an impact on the economic prospects of women, as white women are more likely to attain professional and managerial jobs than are African-American and Hispanic women, and African-American and Hispanic women are more heavily concentrated than are white women in service occupations (Costello and Stone 2001).

The employment patterns of women have resulted in a wage gap between men and women in which women earn, on average, 76 percent of the weekly earnings of men in the same occupational categories. Additionally, unskilled and semi-skilled occupations that are dominated by women pay less than those that are dominated by men. For example, on average, cashiers and apparel sales workers earn less than do truck drivers (Costello and Stone 2001). Employment patterns, differential wages, and divorce all have contributed to the feminization of poverty, in which women head an increasing number of families living below the poverty line. Minority women are disproportionately affected by the feminization of poverty, as 40 percent of black female-headed households and 48 percent of Hispanic female-headed households are poor compared to 28 percent of white female-headed families (Costello and Stone 2001).

The unique experiences of women in relation to the home and the workplace are reflected in their political participation. Scholars note that gender differences in attitudes on social welfare issues are central to understanding the dynamics of the gender gap. Women are consistently more likely than men to believe the government should take a more activist role in assisting the poor and in guaranteeing jobs and a standard of living. Women are also more likely to support increased spending on social services (Shapiro and Mahajan 1986; Andersen 1997; Seltzer, Newman, and Voorhees Leighton 1997; Chaney, Alvarez, and Nagler 1998; Greenberg 1998; Kaufmann and Petrocik 1999). For example, in 1994, following the demise of the Clinton health plan, women were 12.2 percent more likely than men to believe that "it is the government's responsibility to see to it that people have help in paying for doctors and hospital bills" (Seltzer, Newman, and Voorhees Leighton 1997, 27, n. 8). In addition to differences in attitudes on social welfare issues, women are more likely to express feelings of insecurity and pessimism about the general economy and their own personal finances and are less likely than men to support military intervention (Shapiro and Mahajan 1986; Andersen 1997; Seltzer, Newman, and Voorhees Leighton 1997; Chaney, Alvarez, and Nagler 1998; Greenberg 1998; Kaufmann and Petrocik 1999).

On the campaign front, surveys, polls, and experiments concerning voter attitudes indicate that voters do subscribe to certain gender stereotypes, causing them to favor female candidates on compassion issues such as health care, education, children, and the elderly while viewing male candidates as more capable of handling foreign policy and tax issues (Sapiro 1981–82; Alexander and Anderson 1993; Huddy and Terkildsen 1993a, 1993b; Burrell 1994; McDermott 1997). These stereotypes translated into substantive gains for women officeholders in the 1992 elections as the focus on social welfare issues, particularly health care, welfare, and education, in the presidential and congressional campaigns and in the media helped elect more Democratic women (Biersack and Herrnson 1994; Chaney and Sinclair 1994; Schroedel and Snyder 1994; Wilcox 1994; Plutzer and Zipp 1996; Fox 1997; Dolan 2002).

Whether based on socialization patterns, shared experiences, or the expectations of voters, it is clear that women, though divided by race and class, do share common interests. However, it remains an open question whether those interests require the election of more women to achieve full representation in the legislative arena. In order for female legislators to have a distinctive policy impact, the representative must be able to exercise a certain level of independence from her constituents. The level of autonomy appropriate to the representative relationship has long been a subject of debate. The view of the representative as trustee, most famously promoted by Edmund Burke, describes a legislator who is not bound by the wishes of the constituency but uses his or her best judgment to pursue the true interests of his or her constituency and the nation as a whole. At the opposite end of the spectrum, the instructed delegate closely follows the opinions of his or her district and does not take actions that would conflict with those views (Pitkin 1967).

Utilizing elections as an accountability mechanism, the U.S. House of Representatives is designed to favor the selection of delegates rather than trustees. Therefore, the more frequent the elections, the less it matters who is elected because the representative is tied to making decisions that follow the desires of the constituency (Phillips 1998). Indeed, in *Federalist 35*, Alexander Hamilton rejects the assertion that all classes of citizens require their own representatives to guarantee that the House of Representatives will understand and attend to their interests. Instead he explains, "A man who is a candidate for the favor of the people, and who is dependent on the suffrages of his fellow-citizens for the continuance of his public honors, should take care to inform himself of their dispositions and inclinations and should be willing to allow them their proper degree of influence on his conduct" (Rossiter 1961).

Even if it is true that legislators are largely delegates of their electorate following the mandates of their constituencies, past research indicates that the same geographical constituency can support many different reelection constituencies (Fiorina 1974; Fenno 1978). Thus, a female candidate may be more likely to view women as a distinct portion of her reelection constituency, and she may be more likely to attract supporters who are concerned with women's issues (Reingold 1992, 2000; Fox 1997; Thomas 1997; Carroll 2002). For example, moderate Republican Constance Morella's (MD) emphasis on women's issues, including domestic violence, reproductive rights, and child care, has helped her maintain a winning electoral coalition in a district that is heavily Democratic. It is very likely that a Democrat who chooses to emphasize a different mix of issues could also prevail in that district.

Moreover, within the broad constraints of constituency preferences, legislators can choose which policy areas to pursue. Although a liberal Democratic congressman and congresswoman might be equally likely to vote in favor of Congresswoman Mink's gender equity amendment, this result does not explain how the issue emerged on the national agenda in the first place. An intensity of commitment stemming from shared membership in the potentially affected group may make the congresswoman more willing to spend the time, staff resources, and political capital necessary to develop gender-related legislation and lobby for its passage. For example, a staffer to a Democratic congresswoman attributed her representative's interest in childcare issues to the fact that she was the first member of the New York City Council to give birth. "As a working mother with a new baby and no access to child care, her husband told her it cost them more money for her to work."[3] Similarly, moderate Republican Nancy Johnson (CT) explained that when considering a potential policy, she thinks about how the policy will affect women who are homemakers, working women with children at home, and single mothers because she "know(s) a lot more about the shape of women's lives and the pattern of women's lives, so I need to look and see how the public policy will affect those patterns, and how it will help or hurt" (quoted in Dodson et al. 1995, 15–16).

This book contributes to the great debate over the relevance of social identity to the quality of representation by examining whether congresswomen demonstrate a more intense commitment to the pursuit of women's issue legislation and whether women bring a different point of view to the policy debate than do their male partisan colleagues. I also investigate the ways in which the political context and the position of individual legislators within the institution constrain their ability to pursue legislative goals regardless of their stated preferences.

Studying the Policy Impact of Women in Congress

Prior to the 103rd Congress, the paucity of women in Congress made it difficult to systematically examine the policy impact of electing women.

To date, most research on women in Congress has focused on whether gender has a significant impact on congressional roll-call voting behavior. Studies that test whether women are generally more liberal than their male colleagues have had mixed results (Frankovic 1977; Gehlen 1977; Leader 1977; Welch 1985; Burrell 1994; Vega and Firestone 1995; McCarty, Poole, and Rosenthal 1996; Clark 1998). However, other research indicates that gender does exert a significant effect on voting for specific women's issues such as abortion (Tatalovich and Schier 1993; Swers 1998) or a set of women's issues (Burrell 1994; Dolan 1997; Swers 1998).

Yet analyses of roll-call voting only scratch the surface of potential gender differences in legislative participation. As Hall (1996) notes, the position a legislator takes on a roll-call vote represents a revealed preference, but it does not indicate the intensity of that preference. To pursue one bill means to forgo opportunities to participate in others. It is the intensity of the representative's preferences that determines which issues become priorities. Therefore, one must look at the entire legislative process behind the vote to determine which legislators are dedicating their time and resources to the pursuit of women's issue legislation.[4]

Insider accounts of the 103rd Congress and case studies of particular bills have provided some initial evidence that congresswomen are taking the lead in supporting and advocating bills dealing with a range of women's issues including abortion, violence against women, and welfare reform (Boxer 1994; Margolies-Mezvinsky 1994; Dodson et al. 1995; Gertzog 1995; Foerstel and Foerstel 1996; Bingham 1997; Dodson 1997, 1998, 2002; Casey and Carroll 1998). However, the most systematic evidence concerning the legislative participation of women has emerged in studies of state legislatures. These studies indicate that women sponsor more bills concerning women's issues (both social welfare and feminist), women are more likely to consider these bills a priority, and women are more likely to have their bills successfully passed into law (Saint-Germain 1989; Dodson and Carroll 1991; Thomas 1994; Dolan and Ford 1995; Bratton and Haynie 1999).

One striking pattern in the state research is that many of the authors do not adequately consider the impact of partisan and institutional factors on women's participation.[5] The authors find that the level of attention that female legislators devote to women's issues depends on the presence of a women's caucus and the proportion of women in the legislature as they approach a "critical mass" (Saint-Germain 1989;

Berkman and O'Connor 1993; Thomas 1994). According to the organizational theories of Rosabeth Moss Kanter (1977), individuals that constitute a minority within an institution will not be able to express their unique preferences and priorities until their numbers approach a balance with the dominant group.

However, these studies do not address whether women are more likely to sponsor women's issue bills because they are more likely to be Democrats or because they are more likely to sit on social welfare committees that have jurisdiction over many women's issues. Since much of the state research is based on survey data across states and at a given point in time, the researchers also cannot evaluate how changes in the institutional and political contexts—such as membership in the minority or majority party, the openness of the external political climate, and access to committee leadership positions—facilitate or constrain a member's ability to pursue policy preferences based on gender. Recently, scholars have begun to investigate how political and institutional factors affect the ability of legislators to achieve gender-related policy goals (e.g., Norton 1995, 1999, 2002; Tamerius 1995; Rosenthal 1997, 1998; Dodson 1998, 2000; Swers 1998, 2002; Reingold 2000; Pearson 2001). The majority of research on the policy impact of women, including my own, is limited by the fact that we must analyze sex differences in behavior as a proxy for gender differences. Thus we must utilize observed differences based on biology to make inferences about the impact of a social construct, gender.[6]

My research addresses the influence of the political and institutional contexts on the behavior of individual representatives by employing a specially created database that traces women's issue legislation through each stage of the legislative process and a series of interviews with male and female representatives and their staff. The analysis examines how much of the influence attributed to gender is better explained by partisan, ideological, or constituency factors. I also pay special attention to the influence of committee position, particularly how a member's committee assignment and access to leadership positions have an impact on his or her ability to pursue women's issue legislation. By comparing legislative activity on women's issues in the 103rd and 104th Congresses, I am able to evaluate how changes in the institutional and political contexts, such as the Republican Party's ascension to majority status and the ensuing highly polarized and conservative ideological atmosphere, affected the willingness of Republican congresswomen to advocate women's issue legislation.

A Theory of Congresswomen's Impact on Women's Issue Legislation

The ensuing chapters test the hypothesis that congresswomen will be more likely to support and advocate women's issue legislation than will their male partisan colleagues. That is, Democratic women will be more likely to pursue this legislation than will Democratic men and Republican women will be more likely to focus on these bills than will Republican men. The book also examines the ways in which the impact of social identity on legislative choices is limited by the imperatives of party loyalty and institutional position. For the purposes of this study, "women's issues" are defined as issues that are particularly salient to women because they seek to achieve equality for women; they address women's special needs, such as women's health concerns or child care; or they confront issues with which women have traditionally been concerned in their role as caregivers, such as education or the protection of children.

Even if female representatives have a propensity to legislate about women's issues, their efforts are likely to be both magnified and constrained by the institutional incentives that channel the efforts of all members of Congress. Within the institution of Congress, expertise and credibility are two of the most highly valued commodities in the policy-making process (Fenno 1973; Kingdon 1989; Smith and Deering 1990). In fact, the committee system is organized to encourage members to specialize and develop policy expertise in an area so that members outside of the committee can trust the quality of their legislative products (Krehbiel 1991). To meet their public policy and reelection goals, legislators look for opportunities to bring new issues to the policy agenda and to formulate solutions to ongoing problems. To convince other legislators of the merits of their proposals, representatives must be able to command expertise and credibility on the issue. With regard to women's issues, the expertise and credibility that congresswomen can claim through personal experience or a connection with women as a group are assets these women can draw on in committee deliberations and in efforts to sell the policy to the public, relevant interest groups, and congressional colleagues.

However, members' ability to act on women's issues is constrained not only by the policy preferences of the district constituency but also by the legislator's position within the institution. Representatives' access to committee seats and leadership positions as well as their status as a member of the majority or minority party both limit the range of policies representatives can influence and constrain their likelihood of success. In addition, the nature of the political context, particularly the ideological composition of Congress, the configuration of interest groups and public opinion on an issue, and the level of media and public attention to the issue, have an impact on legislators' willingness to expend political capital on women's issues.

Comparing Gender Effects by Issue Area: Definitions

Within the broad area of women's issues, I believe that the importance of gender in a member's decision calculus will vary with the subject matter and policy direction of the bill. The more a policy problem is viewed as directly connected to a politically significant aspect of social identity such as gender, the more likely it is that a legislator will rely on gender considerations to guide policy choices. Therefore, I analyze gender differences in legislative activity on subsets of social welfare, feminist, and antifeminist bills. I expect that gender will play the most significant role in a member's decision to advocate feminist bills and that congresswomen will be less likely than congressmen of the same party to support antifeminist legislation. Furthermore, with respect to social welfare issues, I expect that the impact of gender on the decisions of representatives to pursue such bills will be reduced by other factors including party affiliation, institutional position, and constituency interests.

Feminist bills comprise those bills that seek to achieve role equity or role change for women. In their book, *Women and Public Policies: Reassessing Gender Politics,* Joyce Gelb and Marian Palley explain that "role equity issues are those policies that extend rights now enjoyed by other groups (men, minorities) to women. Role change issues appear to produce change in the dependent female role of wife, mother, and homemaker, holding out the potential of greater sexual freedom and independence in a variety of contexts" (Gelb and Palley 1996, 6). Examples of feminist legislation include bills protecting reproductive rights, expanding family and medical leave, and helping victims of domestic violence or sexual harassment.

Conversely, antifeminist legislation seeks to inhibit role change as a threat to the traditional family. Examples of antifeminist bills include legislation restricting abortion, eliminating affirmative action programs for women, and prohibiting gay marriage.

Social welfare legislation includes both liberal and conservative proposals concerning such issues as welfare, health care, and education. These issues highlight women's traditional role as caregiver. In the past, social welfare issues have served as women's gateway to political participation. For example, in the late nineteenth century, years before women gained the right to vote, members of women's groups such as the General Federation of Women's Clubs and the National Congress of Mothers practiced municipal housekeeping by lobbying the state and federal governments to improve public education and establish mothers' pensions, the precursor to the modern day Aid to Families with Dependent Children (AFDC) and Temporary Assistance to Needy Families (TANF) programs (Skocpol 1992). In the contemporary era, candidates emphasize such issues as education and the expansion of health insurance for children in an effort to reach out to women voters, including the famous "soccer moms" (Carroll 1999).

Exploring the Interaction of Gender and Institutional Factors on the Pursuit of Feminist and Social Welfare Policies

The idea that the role of gender should be most important in the decision to support feminist legislation seems counterintuitive when one considers conventional wisdom concerning congressional behavior. For example, Arnold (1990) notes that representatives are most concerned with traceability. They are eager to claim credit for policies that are popular and distribute benefits widely in their district, such as increased funding for education or the expansion of a highway. However, they are most concerned with blame avoidance when it comes to the more controversial policies, such as reproductive rights and affirmative action programs for women, which often constitute feminist legislation. Indeed, these feminist issues are a component of larger cultural and civil rights debates that are creating conflict within the parties and have the potential to disrupt the traditional cleavages that have divided the Democratic and Republican parties since the 1930s (Carmines and Stimson 1989; Wolbrecht 2000; Sanbonmatsu 2002). Thus, rational legislators should avoid action on feminist legislation and limit themselves to voting on these issues, rather than using their scarce political capital to push through legislation that can galvanize interest groups with strong grassroots bases into campaigning against them in the next election cycle. This is especially true in the current political climate in which interest groups sponsor issue advertisements that focus the public's attention on their favored issue and can take control of the message of the campaign away from the candidates.

Yet the highly controversial nature of these bills necessitates a more intense interest in these policies to encourage a legislator to act as an advocate for feminist issues. It is possible that gender role socialization and a female representative's unique life experiences might make her more sensitive to the importance of these issues. If a member had experience with employment discrimination or the difficulty of obtaining child care, she might view the issue as a more pressing concern that requires a legislative remedy. For example, Congresswoman Marge Roukema (R-NJ) explained her decision to act as the principal Republican advocate for the Family and Medical Leave Act by pointing to her experience caring for her son, who had leukemia. She asked, "What would I have done if not only did I have the tragedy and trauma of caring for my child but also had to worry about losing a job and the roof over my head?" (Duncan and Lawrence 1995). Additionally, issues like women's health and domestic violence highlight women's status as a minority in Congress and may activate a congresswoman's belief that she is representing a national constituency of women.

This empathy produced by shared experiences and identification with the interests of a group is central to the representative relationship. In an institution where groups and causes compete for the limited time and attention of members of Congress, the descriptive representative is more likely to expend political capital and resources championing group interests. For example, while Swain (1993) and Lublin (1997) maintain that African-American and white representatives from districts with high minority populations exhibit similar voting records, Canon (1999) found that the African-American representative displayed a greater intensity of commitment to racial issues as these members were more likely than their white counterparts to act as sponsors, cosponsors, and advocates in floor debate for legislation that was directly related to racial concerns. Moreover, in an institution that relies on negotiation and accommodation to produce policy, the intensity of commitment displayed by the descriptive representative may prevent him or her from compromising on proposals that will have a direct impact on the interests of the group in order to achieve a policy deal. For example, female representatives are disproportionately active in the final floor debates on legislation aimed at restricting reproductive rights (Levy, Tien, and Aved 2002; Cramer Walsh 2002; Dodson 2000).

Another reason to question whether the unique policy impact of electing women will be found on feminist issues is that the gender gap is not related to these issues. Voter surveys do not find significant gender differences in attitudes toward such feminist issues as abortion and the desirability of women's participation in the workforce (Sanbonmatsu 1997, 2002; Seltzer, Newman, and Voorhees Leighton 1997; Kaufmann and Petrocik 1999). However, both pro-choice and pro-life women express a greater intensity of feeling on the abortion issue than men do (Seltzer, Newman, and Voorhees Leighton 1997).

Rather, the gender gap is generally attributed to the fact that women are more likely to favor government spending for the disadvantaged, are less likely to be optimistic about the economy, and are more likely to oppose military intervention (Shapiro and Mahajan 1986; Seltzer, Newman, and Voorhees Leighton 1997; Chaney, Alvarez, and Nagler 1998; Kaufmann and Petrocik 1999). These attitudes reflect concerns that are more likely to be addressed by social welfare legislation, such as expanding access to Medicare or increasing food stamp benefits, rather than by feminist legislation. Consequently, Sanbonmatsu (1997, 2002) reports that both Republican and Democratic pollsters believe that the way to reach women voters is to talk to them about children and families and not about feminist issues such as gender roles or women's status in the workplace.

However, female officeholders should not be equated with female voters. Officeholders face a different incentive structure than the voting public does. As rational legislators, women must compete to find issues on which they can successfully pursue legislation and build a reputation both within the institution and at home with constituents. Thus, a representative searches for policy gaps that need to be filled. Feminist issues are more recent additions to the congressional agenda. Some of these issues, such as pay equity, child support, domestic violence, and sexual harassment, only became part of the public discourse as a result of the women's movement in the 1960s and 1970s (Costain 1992; Wolbrecht 2000; Sanbonmatsu 2002). These issues provide opportunities for a member to carve out a policy niche that can be translated into legislative success within the chamber and opportunities for credit claiming with constituents.

Furthermore, since many feminist issues such as reproductive rights and child-care funding have a disproportionate impact on women as a group, female legislators will be viewed as commanding more expertise and moral authority on these issues, making it more likely that their colleagues will turn to them for policy leadership. Thus, Susan Molinari (R-NY) explained her decision to pursue an amendment to the 1994 Crime Bill concerning sex offenders by citing the need to look for policy gaps that were not being addressed by others and her belief that women who are victims of domestic abuse expect her to understand their plight better "than the guy that you are sitting next to" (Dodson et al. 1995).

In contrast, social welfare issues like education and welfare reform represent an area of policy making to which party realignment theorists point as the main line of cleavage that has structured relations between the Republican and Democratic parties since the New Deal

(Burnham 1970; Sundquist 1983). Therefore, these issues also tap a wider range of partisan, district, and policy concerns than do feminist issues, thereby reducing the significance of gender in a legislator's decision to become active on a bill.

Since these social welfare issues are highly integrated into the congressional agenda and committee jurisdictions, there will be much competition among legislators, regardless of gender, to influence policy on these issues with the advantage going to those with more institutional clout, such as the most senior committee members and committee and subcommittee chairs. These members have greater access to committee staff who have years of experience crafting legislation on these issues. Interest groups seeking to benefit from their committee positions will provide these institutional leaders with additional policy information, making it even more difficult for non–committee members and those with less seniority to gain a seat at the policy-making table. Since few congresswomen have attained the seniority necessary to gain leadership positions on key committees, they are further inhibited in their ability to influence the policy debate on social welfare legislation, regardless of their level of interest in these issues.

The Importance of the Political and Institutional Contexts: Differences between the 103rd and 104th Congresses

The ability of congresswomen to express preferences based on gender is highly dependent on variations in the political and institutional contexts, particularly the identity of the majority party, the relative power of the leadership, the ideological composition of Congress, and the public mood. Policy is not made in a vacuum. Members are highly affected by the demands of their party caucus and leaders as well as the external political climate around them (Rhode 1991; Cox and McCubbins 1993; Sinclair 1995). Comparing legislative behavior in the 103rd and 104th Congresses provides an ideal opportunity to assess how the political and institutional environment impacts the decision calculus of members concerning what kinds of policies to advocate.

Of the two Congresses, the 103rd Congress provided the most favorable environment for the passage of women's issue legislation. The 1992 congressional elections were widely hailed as "The Year of the Woman" and were accompanied by a significant rise in the number of female representatives in the House: from twenty-eight in the 102nd Congress to forty-seven in the 103rd (Center for the American Woman and Politics Fact Sheet 1994).[7] The Clarence Thomas–Anita Hill hearings highlighted the dearth of women in Congress and motivated many women to run for office. Numerous female candidates emphasized social welfare issues such as health care and education in their campaigns, and many openly pointed to the need for a woman's point of view in Congress (Chaney and Sinclair 1994; Wilcox 1994; Fox 1997).

The election of Bill Clinton brought a president who held liberal views on women's issues and benefited from a gender gap. The fact that women's issues were highlighted in both the congressional and presidential campaigns made the agenda particularly open to women's issue proposals. In fact, the first bill to pass the 103rd Congress was the Family and Medical Leave Act, a bill that President George H. Bush vetoed twice. Additionally, unified government after twelve years of Republican presidential rule offered the prospect, if not the result, of smoother passage of legislation. A member who expended scarce political capital developing and lobbying for a women's issue bill was less concerned about facing a presidential veto at the end of the line.

In contrast, many political commentators described the Republican takeover of Congress in 1994 as the revenge of the angry white male (Brown and Scripps 1994; Edmonds and Benedetto 1994). Agenda control shifted from Democrats, who wanted to expand social welfare programs such as national health insurance, to Republicans, particularly the new conservative freshmen, who believed they had an electoral mandate to dismantle the welfare state built by Democrats during the New Deal and the Great Society (Gimpel 1996, Killian 1998). In addition, core Republican constituencies vigorously opposed liberal positions on women's issues, particularly reproductive rights. Feminist groups lost access to party and committee leaders as groups representing Christian conservatives gained the ear of the new Republican leaders. Thus, after the House completed consideration of the Contract with America, Speaker Gingrich and the party leadership promised a vote on each item in the Christian Coalition's Contract with the American Family. This contract included such items as a ban on partial birth abortions, the elimination of funding for domestic and international organizations that provide abortion counseling, the abolition of the Department of Education, and a guarantee of parental rights in the upbringing of children (Tin and Greenwald 1995).[8]

These significant changes in the policy agenda gained strength from Republican efforts to impose party government by concentrating power in the party leadership, particularly Speaker Gingrich's office, and by reducing the independent influence of committees. Perhaps the most important institutional change was Gingrich's decision to reward ideological loyalty over seniority in the committee assignment process.

Gingrich placed new conservative freshman on prestigious committees like Appropriations, Budget, and Commerce, and he elevated conservative loyalists to committee chairs over more senior members. To circumvent the committee process further, Speaker Gingrich created party task forces to handle important policy matters such as Medicare and the elimination of executive departments. These party task forces excluded Democrats from deliberation and further limited the independence of committee leaders (Aldrich and Rhode 1995, 1997, 2000; Evans and Oleszek 1997).

Since most women in the House were Democrats, as members of the minority party, they had very little opportunity to influence the legislative agenda on women's issues. The Republican leadership further reduced the impact of women as a group by defunding legislative service organizations, including the Congressional Caucus for Women's Issues. Thus, Republicans eliminated the extra staff resources that Democratic and moderate Republican women utilized to develop independent omnibus proposals concerning women's health, violence against women, and other issues. The women with the potential to gain a seat at the policy-making table included more senior moderate Republican women and a new group of socially conservative Republican freshman women.

Republican Women and the Influence of the Political and Institutional Contexts

The impact of a restricted party agenda and a powerful party leadership on a member's desire to expend political capital pursuing women's issue bills should be most evident in the behavior of moderate Republican women. As members of the less powerful minority, these women might be willing to defect from their party's standard conservative position to support feminist initiatives on women's issues. However, a change in status to the governing majority from the opposition greatly increases the costs of defection. Majority party membership provides more opportunities to gain leadership positions on committees and to generate action on one's priorities on a range of issues, thus increasing the costs of alienating the party leadership and core party constituencies. To reap the benefits of majority status, Republican women may be willing to downplay their commitment to women's issues in order to make gains on other district and policy priorities that conform more easily to the Republican agenda. I therefore pay special attention in this book to changes in the behavior of Republican women across the two Congresses.

Looking Ahead

The determination of the ways in which women are influencing the congressional policy-making process requires a systematic analysis of the entire legislative process from the agenda-setting phases to the final roll-call votes. Therefore, I created a database that tracks representatives' legislative activity on women's issues across the 103rd and 104th Congresses. The database measures the number of women's issue bills sponsored and cosponsored by each member of the House of Representatives. For those bills that advanced to a committee markup and/or floor debate, the database also captures the number of women's issue amendments members offered to each of the bills in committee and on the House floor as well as members' positions on the final roll-call vote.[9] Using this information, I employ regression analysis to evaluate whether female representatives exhibit a more intense commitment to women's issues at each stage of the legislative process than do their male colleagues even after one accounts for the major partisan, constituency, and institutional factors that influence the policy choices of representatives.

A series of interviews with twenty-eight Democratic and Republican representatives and staff supplement the statistical findings by providing insight into how members determine their legislative priorities and what strategies they employ to achieve their goals on women's issues. To capture the diversity of opinion and activity on women's issues, the interview subjects were chosen to include congressmen and congresswomen, Democrats and Republicans, and conservatives and liberals within each party.[10] Each interview subject served or worked for someone who served in the varying political contexts of the 103rd and 104th Congresses and all subjects worked on one or more women's issue bills.[11] Since interviews generally were not conducted with subjects who had no involvement with women's issues, the interviews cannot provide insight into why certain members do not pursue women's issue legislation.

To guard against biased responses, the interview subjects were not told that the research concerned the policy impact of women in Congress and the term "women's issues" was never used in the questioning. Instead, all subjects received a letter requesting an interview to discuss the general topic of how members develop their legislative priorities, as well as a specific area, such as education or health care, with which the respondent was associated.[12] In the chapters that follow, quotes from the interviews highlight trends found in the statistical analysis and provide insight into representatives' strategic calculations concerning the type of legislation to pursue, the building of coalitions, and the risks and obstacles the legislator faced from his or her party, the opposition party, and outside interest groups.[13]

Chapter 2 focuses on the level of institutional power that congresswomen have achieved individually and as a group. In that chapter, I analyze the roles women play within their political parties and their access to formal positions of power within the party and committee leadership structure. I also evaluate how partisan concerns about the gender gap have affected women's positions within their party conferences.

In chapters 3–7, I examine in a detailed way the differences in representatives' commitment to placing women's issues on the national agenda. I evaluate the influence of identity on legislators' decisions to sponsor and cosponsor women's issue bills, to offer women's issue amendments in committee and on the floor, and to vote in favor of liberal positions on women's issue legislation. The analysis demonstrates that the importance of gender considerations varies by the policy area since gender plays a more central role in the decision to pursue feminist legislation than it does in the pursuit of social welfare legislation. My research also highlights the ways in which political and institutional incentives, such as a legislator's committee assignment or a shift from minority to majority party status, structures the range of choices available to a legislator regardless of his or her abstract preferences. Finally, Chapter 8 summarizes the findings of the study and revisits the question of whether electing more women increases attention to women's issue legislation.

By carefully following a series of women's issue bills through the legislative process, my research demonstrates that, even though congressmen and congresswomen often vote a party line, politically significant social identities like gender do influence the nature of the bills placed on the national agenda and the choices made about those bills. However, the translation of preferences into policy is mediated by the position of members within the institution and their relationship to their party caucus and national party constituencies. Untangling the impact of social identity on policy preferences and legislative choices allows us to consider the implications of the underrepresentation of women and other social groups for the democratic process.

Chapter 2

Women, the Political Parties, and the Gender Gap

In his classic text, *Congressmen in Committees*, Richard Fenno (1973) described the three main goals of members of Congress. Representatives, he concluded, want to win reelection, pursue good public policies, and build influence inside Congress. Because of their small numbers and relative lack of seniority, congresswomen in both parties have found it difficult to achieve access to the upper echelons of party and committee leadership. Yet an increasing recognition of the need for diversity and the desire of both Republicans and Democrats to capitalize on or combat the gender gap has provided elected women with additional opportunities to expand their institutional power and exercise leadership on women's issues.

Women and the Formal Positions of Institutional Power

Prior to the election of Nancy Pelosi as minority whip in October 2001, no woman had attained a position within the highest ranks of party leadership. In the 107th Congress (2001–2), the Democrats also appointed women to head their congressional campaign committees, Nita Lowey (D-NY) in the House and Patty Murray (D-WA) in the Senate, and Republicans continued to elect women to serve in the lower level leadership positions of conference vice-chair and conference secretary. However, to this date, no women have been elected Speaker of the House or majority or minority leader.[1] Similarly, due to their lack of seniority, no women have risen to the chairmanship of the prestigious Appropriations, Ways and Means, Rules, Budget, or Commerce Committees. While the Education and Workforce Committee (formerly known as the Education and Labor Committee) has jurisdiction over a wide range of women's issue legislation, only Edith Green (D-OR, 1955–74) has chaired one of its subcommittees (Gertzog 1995; Kaptur 1996).[2] In the

106th Congress (1999–2000), Nancy Johnson (R-CT) ascended to the chair of the Ways and Means Human Resources Subcommittee, the subcommittee responsible for issues related to the new welfare system, known as Temporary Assistance to Needy Families (TANF). In the 107th Congress, she chairs the panel's Health Subcommittee.

In response to their lack of formal institutional power, many Democratic and moderate Republican women claim that they do feel a special responsibility to represent women in their committee work, and they do lobby male committee leaders to take into account a policy's potential impact on women (Dodson et al. 1995; Dodson 1997, 1998; Casey and Carroll 1998; Carroll 2002). For example, Marge Roukema (R-NJ) explained: "But I have to tell you, when I got to Washington, I found that some of the 'women's issues—the family issues'—weren't being addressed by the men in power. Things like child-support enforcement and women's health issues and family safety issues. It wasn't that the men were opposed to these issues—they just didn't get it. They were not sufficiently aware of them. So I realized, in many important areas—if we women in government don't take action, no one else will" (*Congressional Record* 1999, April 13, H1918-19).

Additionally, in interviews, both Democratic and Republican men and women expressed the belief that women and minorities bring a different perspective to the policy process, and it is important to have these groups at the decision-making table. Many of the Republican and Democratic women who have held party leadership posts also feel a sense of responsibility to represent women. For example, in her congressional memoir, Susan Molinari (R-NY) claimed that she used her position as vice-chair of the Republican conference to act as "the party's champion of women's issues." At the height of the budget-cutting battles of the 104th Congress, she convinced the leadership to increase funding for programs to combat violence against women. When other members rolled their eyes at her suggestions for new women's initiatives, Speaker Gingrich backed her and reminded male members that they could not win the next election without the votes of women (Molinari 1998). Similarly, in the 103rd Congress, Louise Slaughter (D-NY) used her position on the leadership-controlled Rules Committee to make sure the Freedom of Access to Abortion Clinic Entrances Act was placed on the House calendar before the end of the session and to push a favorable rule through a committee whose members were largely pro-life (Dodson et al. 1995). Barbara Kennelly (D-CT), who served as a chief deputy whip in the 102nd (1991–92) and 103rd (1993–94) Congresses and conference vice-chair in the 104th (1995–96) Congress, said that "women have a different perspective and you need women to be in the room to make sure it is heard. I worked on women and children's issues over and above committee work, constituent service, and case work."[3]

While both Democratic and Republican women agree that it is important to have women at the table because females bring a different perspective to policy making, Democratic women are more willing to challenge their party leadership explicitly and demand that women be considered for positions because of their gender. According to one Republican staffer, "Republican women do not overtly promote themselves as women" or argue "that we need more women, . . . the Republican Party in general sees a need but it is not overly stated." Since the 104th Congress, when Susan Molinari (R-NY) was elected conference vice-chair and Barbara Vucanovich (R-NV) became conference secretary, a "consensus has developed that women should be elected to these positions and the people competing for these positions in the 105th (1997–98) and 106th (1999–2000) Congresses were largely women." This pattern of women competing for the lower rungs of the Republican leadership continued in the 107th Congress when Deborah Pryce (R-OH) advanced from conference secretary to vice-chair and Republicans elected Barbara Cubin (R-WY) from a field of three women to serve as conference secretary (Foerstel 2000a, 2000b).

On the Democratic side, the more liberal ideological views espoused by the Democratic Party incline members of the caucus to arguments based explicitly on the need for diversity. For example, throughout her campaign to replace David Bonior as whip when he retires in January 2002, Nancy Pelosi maintained that women "deserve a seat at the leadership table" (Earle 2002). She also argued that her election would allow the party to bring a "fresh face" to the public and would increase the party's advantage with women voters (Foerstel 2001a, 2001b). Similarly, when the position of chief deputy whip became vacant in 1991, Speaker Thomas Foley responded to pressure from women, blacks, and conservative Southerners, all of whom felt excluded from party decision making, by dividing the position into three chief deputy whip posts and appointing a member of each of the three underrepresented groups (Foerstel and Foerstel 1996).

At the opening of the 106th Congress, when Congresswoman Rosa DeLauro (D-CT) failed to win a race for conference chair, the Democratic congresswomen rebelled about the absence of women in the elected Democratic leadership, pointing out that Republicans had elected women to serve as conference vice-chair and conference secretary. Interviews with Democratic legislators and staff revealed that after DeLauro lost the election for conference chair, a Democratic congressman who is also a statistician approached Carolyn Maloney (D-NY), the chair of the Congressional Caucus for Women's Issues, and showed her a chart he had compiled indicating the percentage of women on the various House committees. The tables revealed that a large percentage of women serve on committees like Agriculture and Science, while few women have seats on the prestigious committees, such as Commerce and Ways and Means. Democratic women then organized and demanded a meeting with Minority Leader Richard Gephardt (D-MO) in which they urged him to appoint more women to fill openings on powerful committees and to include more women in the leadership. In response, Gephardt created a new position, assistant to the minority leader, and DeLauro was appointed to the post. Democratic women, African-Americans, Hispanics, and conservative "blue dogs" continue to rely on the need for diversity as they compete to fill the numerous leadership posts that will be open in the 108th (2003–4) Congress. These positions will include the conference chair and vice-chair positions, which are limited to two terms. In addition, Nancy Pelosi could vacate the whip post and ascend to the position of party leader if Richard Gephardt becomes Speaker or resigns to run for president in 2004 (Foerstel 2001a, 2001b).[4]

The Gender Gap and Informal Paths to Institutional Power

Although seniority rules have slowed congresswomen's rise to positions of power in the committees and party leadership, partisan concerns over the potential impact of the gender gap have facilitated women's efforts to raise their profile within their respective party caucuses and to take the lead on gendered issues. Since Republicans seized control of Congress from the Democrats in 1994, they have lost House seats in each succeeding election, and in the 107th Congress their majority control rests on only a six-seat margin. In an era of such tight party competition, party leaders make extra efforts to develop and advertise policy proposals that will attract specific groups of voters and, therefore, both parties are targeting women voters. Although the gender gap is small, women have slightly favored the Democrats since the late 1960s (Seltzer, Newman, and Voorhees Leighton 1997). The gender gap widened in 1996, when 54 percent of women supported Bill Clinton in contrast to only 43 percent of men and when the media focused on the voting behavior of the "soccer mom" (Carroll 1999; Kaufmann and Petrocik 1999).[5] Additionally, in 1996, more women voted than men—with 56 percent of women turning out to vote compared to 53 percent of men. The higher turnout among women helped Democrats reclaim House seats in 1996 and 1998 (Kirchhoff 1999). While the Florida recount and the divergence between the popular and Electoral College votes made the 2000 elections a unique historical event, the gender gap continued at the same magnitude, as Al Gore received 12 percent more votes from women than from men. Similarly, across the country, women favored Democratic House candidates, creating a nine-point gender gap, and women helped elect more Democratic women to the Senate (Center for the American Woman and Politics 2000).

In response to these trends, Democrats are designing their policy proposals and public appeals with an eye toward maintaining women's support, while Republicans actively work to expand their appeal among women. To achieve these goals, party leaders have increasingly turned to women to act as spokespersons on women's, children's, and family issues and to take a leading role in legislative battles on women's issues. As one Republican congressman complained, "The Democrats will do whatever they can to expand the gender gap." Democratic members and staffers agreed that the party does encourage women to be out in front at press conferences, presidential bill-signing ceremonies, and floor debate on women's issues. As one Democratic staffer explained the dynamic, "The parties are sensitive to the gender gap so they want to appeal to women, children, and family issues. As long as the parties focus on these issues to capture the women's vote, it helps women in office who can be leaders on these issues."

The debates over gun control during the 106th Congress highlight the Democratic strategy. A series of high-profile school shootings brought the issue of gun control back into the public spotlight. Democratic Party polling demonstrated that women care more about gun control legislation than men do and that women are more likely to let their votes be influenced by a candidate's position on gun control. Therefore, Democrats began framing their discussions of gun control in terms of child safety rather than crime, with the presumption that the phrase will resonate especially strongly with women voters. Three Democratic Congresswomen, Carolyn McCarthy (D-NY), Nita Lowey (D-NY), and Assistant Minority Leader Rosa DeLauro (D-CT), took the lead in organizing press conferences, lobbying colleagues, and counting votes to limit Democratic defectors and to attract Republican support for the McCarthy-Roukema Amendment, which would add gun control provisions to a juvenile justice bill. As the congresswomen explained, they "stepped to the foreground of an issue they had long been passionate about and party leaders almost immediately encouraged them to stay there" (Bruni 1999). Indeed, the murder of her husband and injury of her son in a mass shooting on the Long Island Railroad propelled Congresswoman McCarthy to run for office in the first place. After the House defeated the McCarthy-Roukema Amendment in June 1999, the Democratic women organized a floor protest by lining up to make procedural requests to revise and extend their remarks (Carney 1999). In the weeks following the amendment's defeat, Democratic congresswomen used the unconstrained floor time provided by the period for one-minute speeches at the opening of the legislative day to read the names of children who had been killed as a result of gun violence (e.g., see *Congressional Record* 1999, September 24, H8632–33).

As Democrats turn to congresswomen to expand their support among women voters, Republicans, particularly in the 104th Congress, deploy women in a more defensive manner. Discussing her role as conference vice-chair, Susan Molinari described one of her duties as "putting the friendly face on Republican issues," particularly when Republicans feared that Democrats and President Clinton would portray their policies as unfriendly to women in the battle for public opinion (Molinari 1998). Another Republican staffer close to the leadership explained that "the Republican leaders will ask women to speak when they know the Democrats will have their women out to demagogue an issue. By having women speak at a press conference or in the floor debate, they get women to put a smiley, soft face on issues and prevent Republicans from looking like mean ogres. This happened most often in the 104th and 105th Congresses on welfare reform and other Contract with America items. In the 106th, they [Republicans] have not introduced much extreme legislation. They are not trying to dismantle departments or overhaul social legislation."

In addition to deploying women to protect their policies from Democratic attack, Republicans rely on congresswomen's instant credibility as women to label certain feminist policies supported by Democrats as unnecessary and to bolster some antifeminist proposals. For example, Republicans called on women to deny the need for federal funding of vocational programs for displaced homemakers in the 105th Congress and gender equity in education legislation in the 106th Congress. Similarly, a Republican congressman explained that when the leaders agreed to allow him to attach his bill eliminating federal affirmative action programs to a transportation reauthorization bill, he asked a moderate Republican woman to sponsor the amendment. He turned to this particular woman, who was not on the committee of jurisdiction, because "she had been interested in and supportive on the issue in the past" and he believed "she could bring other moderates on board and show that it is not just a white guy from—pushing the issue." Furthermore, Republican leaders originally were reluctant to allow the amendment "because he is a white guy from—with few minorities in [his] district."

Other legislators and staffers explained that, in an effort to narrow the gender gap, Republicans also actively seek out women's issue bills that will improve their standing with women and draw attention away from abortion. As a result, party and committee leaders, often prodded by Republican women, have advanced proposals on such issues as breast cancer, child abuse, violence against women, adoption, and foster care. Since the 104th Congress, Republicans have also made efforts to repackage traditional Republican policies on taxes and other fiscal issues in ways that will attract women. In the 105th and 106th Congresses, Republicans courted women by seeking legislation to eliminate the marriage penalty and protect innocent spouses, often divorced women, who are liable for tax debts resulting from the actions of their former spouses (Wells 1998). Jennifer Dunn (R-WA), who leads Republican efforts to bridge the gender gap, utilizes press conferences and public speeches to explain how tax issues affect women (Kirchhoff 1999). Her congressional Web site includes a special section for women that lists Republican accomplishments on behalf of women and explains how issues like estate taxes disproportionately affect women since, on average, they outlive men.

Working under the assumption that women will listen to other women, Republicans increasingly spotlight female legislators to reach out to women voters. For example, in both 1999 and 2000, women who were not members of the top House and Senate Republican leadership received the honor of delivering the nationally televised Republican response to President Clinton's State of the Union Address. Jennifer Dunn (R-WA) and former football star Steve Largent (R-OK) delivered the response in 1999, while Senators Susan Collins (R-ME) and Bill Frist (R-TN) spoke in 2000.[6] To prepare for the 2002 elections, Republicans launched a comprehensive outreach effort to attract women voters that included a Web site entitled "Winning Women," which advertises Republican policies that help women, highlights the activities of Republican women in Congress and the Bush administration, and encourages women to run for office on a Republican ticket (Edsall 2001). For example, the Web site recently featured a three-part series on freshman Congresswoman Melissa Hart (R-PA), which highlighted her legislative efforts on behalf of women, including bills she sponsored to reduce the number of abandoned infants, to fund job-training programs for victims of domestic violence and other displaced homemakers, and to protect children from Internet pornographers (www.winningwomen.org).

The Parties and Women's Institutional Power: Symbolic or Real?

At first glance, Democratic and Republican efforts to highlight women in public debates might be dismissed as mere symbolism. In her study of skewed groups, in which there is a large preponderance of one type of member over another, Kanter (1977) found that in such groups more numerous "dominants" shape the culture and control group decisions. Dominants treat members of the minority as "tokens" who "represent" their category, as symbols rather than as individuals. Indeed some congresswomen, particularly Republican women, expressed a concern that they did not want to be pigeonholed as exponents of certain women's issues. Pro-life women mentioned this problem most often, asserting that even though they support the pro-life position, if they responded to all the requests from interest groups, party and committee leaders, and individual sponsors to speak on the issue, abortion would be the only issue with which they were visibly identified. Another staffer to a Republican congresswoman asserted that her representative is very active on children's issues, sponsoring legislation and speaking on the floor and at press conferences. However, she is concerned about being branded as a single-issue legislator and is currently seeking opportunities to move away from children's issues in order to expand her legislative profile.

There may be an element of tokenism in the parties' employment of congresswomen to reach out to women voters, yet most congresswomen and their staff view the current dynamics as an opportunity to gain institutional power for themselves, focus attention on issues they care about, and build support among congressmen who want to reach out to women voters. All members look to build a legislative niche in which they are perceived as experts on an issue and can point to tangible legislative accomplishments in their bids for reelection. As one staffer explained, "The goal of a member is to get so well known on an issue that you are the person people, both interest group representatives and other members, come to first." Many congresswomen believe that their life experiences and the credibility they command on women's issues helps them to insert themselves into important policy debates and provides them with opportunities to move forward in the party conference.

Indeed, another staffer maintained that when the parties ask women to step forward as spokespersons or legislative leaders on women's issues, the congresswomen are "happy to do it because it brings them prominence and it allows them to do a favor for the leadership. Members want to collect these favors so they can cash them in later." For example, Jennifer Dunn's efforts to expand the Republican Party's appeal among women have helped her to promote herself in the Republican Party caucus and have catapulted her into leadership circles. She served as conference secretary and vice-chair in the 105th Congress, and in the 106th Congress, she was considered a serious candidate for majority leader (Katz 1998). During the 2000 presidential election she served as one of the chairs of the Republican national convention that launched the general election campaign of George W. Bush.

By contrast, another staffer who works for a moderate Republican woman who has defected from her party on certain high-profile issues like managed care, gun control, and abortion claimed that her congresswoman will speak against gender equity legislation because "she does not believe women need help to succeed and by taking the Republican banner on this issue she can make them look good and can build up chips to gain leeway when she defects on other issues." Thus, one congresswoman used her gender to promote herself within the party leadership while another used gender to reduce the risk of sanctions when she defects from her party's position on other issues.

The differences between these two congresswomen also highlight the fact that, regardless of gender, legislators will not be accorded positions of prominence unless their beliefs on an issue reflect the majority opinion within their party's caucus. Since they gained the majority, Republicans have elevated the importance of ideological loyalty. In the 104th Congress, Gingrich and the Republican leadership abandoned the traditional reliance on seniority to appoint more conservative members to chair committees, and they placed a six-year term limit on chairs (Evans and Oleszeck 1997; Aldrich and Rhode 2000). When this term limit took effect in the 107th Congress, Republican leaders again emphasized allegiance to party goals over seniority as aspiring chairmen auditioned in front of the Republican Steering Committee. The shift away from strict reliance on seniority is a potential obstacle to the ambitions of moderate Republican legislators, as evidenced by the fact that despite her standing as the most senior member of the committee, Marge Roukema (R-NJ) failed in her 2001 bid to become chair of the Financial Services Committee. Recognizing the potential public relations problem created by excluding women from the roster of committee chairs, the leadership convinced the new Bush administration to offer Roukema the position of U.S. Treasurer, a position with very limited authority. However, she refused the appointment (Eilperin 2001; Foerstel and Ota 2001).

The importance of party loyalty is equally significant in the Democratic Caucus. As one conservative Democratic congressman complained, "If you are going to be socially conservative and pursue your convictions, you cannot have leadership ambitions. To move up in leadership or into the Senate within the Democratic Party, you must move left. For instance, the current minority leader [Dick Gephardt (D-MO)] used to be pro-life and pro-aid to the Contras." Similarly, while pro-choice congresswomen always lead the Democrats in abortion debates on the floor and at press conferences, the few pro-life Democratic women never speak on the floor or in the media. As the congressman explained, "The party does not keep them quiet; it is a personal choice, since they don't reflect the majority opinion within the caucus on the issue, they don't want to draw attention to themselves." Thus, the parties' desire to reach out to women voters provides opportunities to expand institutional power and assume legislative leadership for those congresswomen who agree with their party's position on specific issues.

The Role of the Congressional Caucus for Women's Issues

While partisan concerns over the gender gap have helped individual women to amass institutional power, over time the Congressional Caucus for Women's Issues (CCWI) has helped congresswomen as a group to draft legislative proposals and build support for those initiatives. The CCWI reached the height of its influence in the Democrat-controlled 103rd Congress, when it was described as a player on specific women's issues (Dodson et al. 1995; Gertzog 1995; Foerstel and Foerstel 1996). Although the caucus is bipartisan, Democratic women constitute the most active members and Republicans perceive it as a liberal group. At the end of the 103rd Congress, the caucus newsletter touted a record sixty-six measures passed to improve the lives of women and their families (Congressional Caucus for Women's Issues 1994). Caucus members and staff put together omnibus legislative packages on women's health, gender equity in education, and economic equity (including such issues as pensions and pay equity). Group members successfully persuaded the relevant Democratic committee chairmen to include their bill provisions on women's health and gender equity in education in both the appropriations process and reauthorization bills for the National Institutes of Health, the Elementary and Secondary Education Act, and other programs (Congressional Caucus for Women's Issues 1994; Gertzog 1995).

When Republicans ascended to majority power in the 104th Congress, they defunded all legislative service organizations and the caucus lost its funding and the accompanying staff. The group had no influence on the Republican agenda because Republicans viewed it as a liberal organization, and few Republican women joined the caucus. In the 105th Congress, the group began to rebuild when its cochairs, Eleanor Holmes Norton (D-DC) and Nancy Johnson (R-CT), convinced almost all congresswomen to join the group, and the chairs worked to develop a consensus agenda around issues such as women's health, child support, and women-owned businesses while dropping any reference to abortion (Kirchhoff 1999). Some staffers complained that the effort to develop consensus positions on which all congresswomen can agree makes the caucus platform too general. However, the caucus is still perceived as a place where congresswomen can exchange information and network for support for their legislation. Some legislators believe that its endorsement is still valuable for developing public support for legislation. Thus, the creation of the caucus helped women expand their influence beyond their small numbers; however the value of the caucus as a tool for legislative influence is highly dependent on Democratic control of Congress.

Conclusion

In the final analysis, congresswomen's junior status has limited their access to the formal positions of institutional power such as committee chairmanships and party leadership posts. However, congresswomen have expanded their institutional clout by focusing the attention of party leaders on the need for diversity at the policy-making table. In addition, the desire of party leaders to attract women voters has provided many individual congresswomen with an opportunity to gain public prominence and exercise legislative leadership on all types of legislation. Yet the value of this avenue to institutional power will fluctuate with the visibility of the "gender gap" in the electorate, as congressional leaders are responsive to proposals that they believe will attract a swing voting population. Finally, the Congressional Caucus for Women's Issues provides congresswomen with an opportunity to develop legislation, exchange information, and cooperate across party lines. However, the fortunes of the caucus fluctuate with Democratic Party control. The elimination of the caucus staff by the Republican Party and the Republican perception of the caucus as a liberal group have reduced the group's policy influence. Thus, while congresswomen can utilize the caucus and partisan concerns over the gender gap as instruments to promote their legislative goals and advance their position within the institution, these mechanisms cannot substitute for the traditional avenues to power, particularly seniority and access to committee leadership posts.

In the ensuing chapters, I closely examine the legislative behavior of representatives to determine whether women are more committed to the pursuit of women's issues. By comparing legislative activity in the 103rd and 104th Congresses, I illuminate the ways in which changes in the political context and a member's position within the institution alter his or her decision calculus concerning what type of policies to pursue. For example, do women utilize their positions on pivotal subcommittees to advance gender-related legislation? How does ascension to the majority, with social conservatives as a key element of the majority coalition, affect the willingness of moderate Republican women to support feminist policy initiatives? These questions can only be answered by a careful examination of the choices of representatives at each stage of the legislative process.

Chapter 3

Bill Sponsorship:
Placing Women's Issues
on the National Agenda

Among the thirty-eight bills introduced during the 106th Congress by a northern Democratic congresswoman are a group concerning the conduct of the 2000 Census that reflect her committee responsibilities and several bills that help certain important business and consumer interests in her district. However, the congresswoman's list of bills also includes proposals to expand the availability of child care and to initiate research on the extent to which dioxin and other additives in tampons contribute to reproductive diseases in women. She has also sponsored a series of bills to protect women who breastfeed from employment discrimination and to provide tax credits to employers to encourage them to set up private, sanitary lactation areas. When asked about these breastfeeding and tampon safety bills, the congresswoman's legislative director replied, "She is ahead of the curve on [bringing attention to] these issues. Ten to fifteen years ago people would not talk about breast cancer on the floor. They did not want to mention breasts. Now everybody wants to help on breast cancer. We have gotten articles in *USA Today* and the *Wall Street Journal* on these issues and she is getting a lot of cosponsors."

The legislative director's comments demonstrate that bill sponsorship is an important tool that legislators use in their quest to gain attention for issues and ultimately to see their proposals incorporated into law. Analysis of patterns of bill sponsorship in Congress thus provides important insights about which members are working to place women's interests on the national agenda. In contrast to other legislative activities, like floor amending in which restrictive rules governing floor debate can prevent members from offering women's issue proposals, representatives have complete control over the number and content of the bills they sponsor. By evaluating the role of gender in the decisions of representatives to sponsor women's issue bills, this chapter takes a first step toward determining whether congresswomen are more interested in pursuing women's issue legislation than are their male partisan colleagues.

Why Do Members Sponsor Legislation?

Representatives sponsor bills for a variety of reasons ranging from an interest in promoting good public policy to pure reelection considerations (Schiller 1995). On the public policy side, members sponsor bills to demonstrate their expertise on an issue and to develop support for their initiatives. For example, a member may sponsor a bill on Medicare reform to establish him- or herself as an expert on health issues so he or she will be included in the policy debate when Congress tackles the Medicare crisis. A staffer to a congresswoman who sponsored several bills to expand family and medical leave maintained that the congresswoman knows that these bills will not go anywhere while the Republicans control the majority. However, if the Democrats regain control, she "will already have a bill on it so she will be seen as an expert and will be able to be a leader, a player on the issue."

Alternatively, a member may sponsor a bill to draw attention to an issue or to shore up the support of relevant interest groups. For example, a Republican subcommittee staffer explained that one congressman sponsors a human life amendment in every Congress even though he does not expect it to go anywhere. He continuously introduces this bill to draw attention to the pro-life position and to tell interested groups that ideally, this is what he would do if he had the support in Congress.

Interest groups seek to bolster the prospects of their proposals by recruiting a sponsor who is a leader or high-ranking member on the committee with jurisdiction over the legislation. For example, a staffer to a Democratic member of the Judiciary Committee complained that, while his congressman is very active on hate crimes and the Hate Crimes Bill is very important to the homosexual community in his district, the interest groups wanted the Judiciary Committee chair and ranking member to sponsor the bill.

Outside the chamber, interest groups will seek out a particular sponsor to capitalize on his or her moral authority on an issue. The fate of the Child Custody Protection Act exemplifies this strategy. During the 105th Congress, the National Right to Life Committee recruited a Republican congresswoman to sponsor this bill, which prohibits the transportation of a minor across state lines in order to avoid state parental consent laws concerning abortion. Although the congresswoman was not a member of the committee with jurisdiction over the legislation and many pro-life legislators would be willing to sponsor this high-profile bill, the group approached the congresswoman because of her moral authority. They wanted a female sponsor who could draw the connection to motherhood and counter the common perception that all women are pro-choice.[1]

On the electoral side, members sponsor bills to demonstrate that they are working for their constituents' interests. Representatives' Web sites and newsletters overflow with information about the bills they have sponsored to address the issues that preoccupy their constituents. Staffers noted that if a representative is asked about what he or she is doing on an issue, it is helpful to be able to point to a bill he or she sponsored. Also, members sponsor bills to appeal to a specific group of voters during an election year or to immunize themselves against criticism from an opponent. For example, Dodson (1997) reports that Republican party leaders assigned a popular amendment, which would protect victims of domestic violence from discrimination by insurance companies, to a Republican congressman who was in a difficult reelection fight and needed a women's issue. Similarly, a Democratic staffer explained, "If the leadership wants to help you, they will give you a high-profile bill or amendment to sponsor so you can get media coverage in your district." Thus, depending on legislators' goals, their bill sponsorship patterns will reflect varying levels of commitment toward women's issues. An analysis of bill sponsorship is therefore a good first step toward determining which members are working to bring women's issues to the national agenda.

The Women's Issue Bill Database

To evaluate which members are most interested in gender-related legislation, I created a database that measures the number of women's issue bills sponsored by each representative during the 103rd and 104th Congresses. Women's issues are defined as bills that are particularly salient to women because they seek to achieve equality for women; they address women's special needs, such as women's health concerns or child-care issues; or they confront issues with which women have traditionally been concerned in their role as caregivers, such as education or the protection of children. However, when identifying which specific bills concern women's issues, one can find reasons to categorize all bills as women's issues or no bills as women's issues. To identify a reasonable sample that can be duplicated, I employed the monthly legislative reports of five major liberal and conservative women's groups. Each group claims to represent women's interests and has a legislative department devoted to following women's issues in Congress. The liberal groups include the American Association of University Women and the National Organization for Women. Concerned Women for America and Eagle Forum are conservative groups associated with the religious right. The Congressional Caucus for Women's Issues (later reconfigured as Women's Policy, Inc.) is a bipartisan but liberal-leaning congressional caucus devoted to the promotion of women's, children's, and family issues. When the new Republican majority defunded legislative service organizations including CCWI, the staff of CCWI formed Women's Policy, Inc., a think thank devoted to providing nonpartisan research and information on legislative actions affecting women and families.[2]

To ensure that there is no systematic bias in the sample, I reviewed the approximately five thousand bill synopses per Congress, which describe the bills proposed by each Republican and Democratic member. While I was concerned that this method would overrepresent the influence of congresswomen and Democrats, I did not find either of these biases. After reviewing the bill summaries, I supplemented the sample by adding bills that matched the subject areas identified by the women's groups. For example, in the 103rd Congress, the women's groups identified eleven bills concerning adoption and foster care. The review of the bill synopses revealed eight additional bills on this topic, which were then included in the sample. The final sample contains 510 bills sponsored by 195 representatives for the 103rd Congress and 569 bills proposed by 224 members for the 104th Congress. The samples make up about 10 percent of all bills introduced in the 103rd Congress and 14 percent of the bills offered in the 104th Congress, excluding resolutions.[3]

To provide a general picture of the sample, figures 1 and 2 divide the bills into eight major issue categories: children and families (non-education), education, civil rights/affirmative action, economic equity and employment benefits, women's health, general health, crime, and welfare.[4] In their efforts to influence the direction of policy and reassure their constituents, members will sponsor numerous pieces of legislation. However, very few bills actually advance through the policy process. In fact, only ninety bills in the 103rd Congress and eighty-seven bills in the 104th Congress, approximately one-fifth of the samples, saw some action beyond referral to a committee. Action ranges from subcommittee hearings to passage into law. Thus, in the 103rd Congress, legislators sponsored 135 bills on children and family issues including adoption, foster care, child abuse, children's health, tax credits for caregivers of

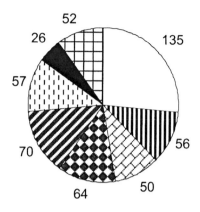

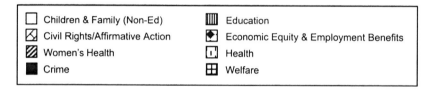

Figure 1   The 103rd Congress: Women's Issue Bills by Subject Area

NOTE: 195 members sponsored 510 bills. Some of the bills could be placed in more than one category. For example, the crime category includes some bills dealing with crimes against children. However, in this graph none of the bills are double counted. Therefore, one should not draw conclusions about interest in specific subject areas based on this graph.

elderly relatives, elimination of the marriage penalty, crimes against children, services for at-risk youth, child support, and child care. However, only 13 percent, or seventeen bills, advanced to even a subcommittee hearing and only eleven bills became law or were incorporated into larger bills that became law.

Finally, to evaluate whether the influence of gender on the sponsorship decisions of legislators varies by policy area, I divided the full sample of women's issue bills into subsets of feminist, social welfare, and antifeminist bills. Among the subsets of women's issue bills, examples of feminist bills offered in the 103rd and 104th Congresses include bills protecting reproductive rights, expanding family and medical leave, increasing funding for women's health research, protecting victims of domestic violence or sexual harassment, creating programs for women-owned businesses, establishing gender equity programs in education, enforcing child-support laws, and increasing access to child care for welfare recipients.

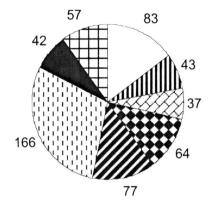

Figure 2 The 104th Congress: Women's Issue Bills by Subject Area

NOTE: 224 members sponsored 569 bills. Some of the bills could be placed in more than one category. For example, the health category includes some bills dealing with children's health. However, in this graph none of the bills are double counted. Therefore, one should not draw conclusions about interest in specific subject areas based on this graph.

In contrast to the feminist bills that promote role equity and/or role change for women, antifeminist bills seek to inhibit role change as a threat to the traditional family (Gelb and Palley 1996). Most of the antifeminist bills introduced in the 103rd and 104th Congresses concern efforts to hinder abortion. Other examples include bills prohibiting funding for international family planning programs, eliminating sex education programs in schools, outlawing gay marriage, prohibiting homosexuals from serving in the military, eliminating affirmative action programs for women and minorities, and requiring welfare recipients to disclose the paternity of the child in order to receive benefits.

The social welfare bills include both liberal and conservative proposals concerning issues with which women have historically been concerned in their role as caregiver, such as health care, education, and poverty assistance. Examples of social welfare bills sponsored during the 103rd and 104th Congresses include proposals to expand health insurance coverage, reform Medicare, expand coverage of mental health

Table 1 Women's Issue Bill Sponsorship in the 103rd and 104th Congresses

Issue Type	103rd Congress (N = 433)		104th Congress (N = 430)	
	No. of Members Who Sponsor	No. of Bills	No. of Members Who Sponsor	No. of Bills
All women's issues	195	510	224	569
Feminist	99	221	82	175
Social welfare	138	264	176	351
Antifeminist	11	14	29	44

NOTE: In the 103rd Congress, a group of eleven bills concerning the "nanny tax" were included in the full set of women's issues but were not assigned to any of the policy categories. In the 104th Congress, separate sections of an omnibus bill sponsored by Barbara Vucanovich (R-NV) were counted in the feminist and antifeminist categories.

services, increase funding for school lunches, create school choice voucher programs, establish regulations for foster care or adoption, punish crimes against children and the elderly, and reform welfare.

Table 1 lists the number of members sponsoring each subset of bills and the number of bills introduced in each policy area. It is important to notice that most legislators do not sponsor any women's issue bills. In fact, only in the 104th Congress does the percentage of members sponsoring women's issue bills reach 50 percent. Among those members who do pursue women's issue initiatives, more representatives focus their energy on social welfare legislation than on either feminist or antifeminist proposals. The patterns revealed in table 1 naturally raise the question of whether electing more women will lead to more attention to gender-related legislation.

Uncovering Gender Differences in Bill Sponsorship

As a first step toward determining whether congresswomen are more likely to support and advocate gender-related legislation than are their male partisan colleagues, I cross-tabulated the bill sponsorship data by gender and party. The results in tables 2 and 3 reveal several striking patterns in legislators' bill-sponsorship behavior. First, the tables clearly demonstrate the importance of majority party status to a member's level of activity on women's issues. A focus on the absolute number of bills sponsored in each Congress indicates that Democratic and Republican men and women all sponsored more women's issue bills when their party held power, with Democrats reducing the number of women's issue bills they sponsored from the 103rd to the 104th Congress, while

Table 2   The 103rd and 104th Congresses: Women's Issue Bill Sponsorship

	Democratic Men (103rd $N = 222$; 104th $N = 165$)		Democratic Women (103rd $N = 36$; 104th $N = 31$)		Republican Men (103rd $N = 163$; 104th $N = 217$)		Republican Women (103rd $N = 12$; 104th $N = 17$)	
	Sponsor (%)	Bills	Sponsor (%)	Bills	Sponsor (%)	Bills	Sponsor (%)	Bills
103rd Congress	45	220	72	134	37	111	83	45
104th Congress	54	173	77	111	47	229	59	56

NOTE: N = Number of members in the category. Thus, there were 222 male Democrats serving in the 103rd Congress.

Table 3   The 103rd and 104th Congresses: Feminist, Social Welfare, and Antifeminist Bill Sponsorship

Issue Type	Democratic Men (103rd $N = 222$; 104th $N = 165$)		Democratic Women (103rd $N = 36$; 104th $N = 31$)		Republican Men (103rd $N = 163$; 104th $N = 217$)		Republican Women (103rd $N = 12$; 104th $N = 17$)	
	% Sponsor	No. of Bills	% Sponsor	No. of Bills	% Sponsor	No. of Bills	% Sponsor	No. of Bills
103rd Congress:								
Feminist	23	88	58	72	12	29	75	32
Social welfare	33	128	47	59	26	64	42	13
Antifeminist	<1	1	0	0	6	13	0	0
104th Congress:								
Feminist	19	39	65	70	11	43	35	23
Social welfare	44	133	52	41	36	146	59	31
Antifeminist	1	1	0	0	12	40	12	3

NOTE: N = Number of members in the category. Thus, there were 222 male Democrats serving in the 103rd Congress.

Republicans increased their sponsorship activity from the 103rd to the 104th Congress.[5] This result stems from the fact that majority party status translates into agenda control and responsibility. Majority legislators know that their party leaders and committee chairs determine which bills will receive attention in committee and on the floor. Therefore, representatives increase their sponsorship rates when they believe they have an opportunity to shape policy outcomes and to see their proposals enacted into law.

In addition to the importance of majority/minority relations, the results in table 2 also reflect the upheaval in the political context created by the shift of power from Democrats to Republicans in the 104th

Congress. The impact of the changing power dynamics is most striking in the behavior of men as the percentage of Republican and Democratic men who sponsored women's issue bills increased by approximately 10 percent. After forty years in the minority, Republicans believed they had a mandate to dismantle the welfare state built up during the New Deal and the Great Society. Accordingly, they concentrated their attention on reforming social programs such as AFDC, Medicare, and Medicaid—areas that hold important implications for women. One Republican staffer involved in the welfare reform debate attributed Republicans' increased attention to social welfare issues to a combination of the responsibilities of majority status and the election of more social conservatives. According to this staffer, in the past, Republicans had "ceded many social welfare issues to the Democrats because these programs are not natural Republican interests, they have not developed the expertise on these issues and they prefer to focus on things like taxes and trade. Conservatives did not get involved in social issues until the social conservatives came to Congress and Republicans got the majority." Responding to the new political holy war, larger proportions of Democratic men and women offered legislation to gain entry into the debate and to protect their favored programs.

The data in table 2 clearly indicate that, within each party, women are more likely to sponsor women's issue bills than are their male colleagues. Across both Congresses, between 23 percent and 27 percent more Democratic women than Democratic men utilized their scarce resources of time, staff, and political capital on the development of women's issue legislation. Among Republicans, 83 percent of Republican women sponsored a women's issue bill in the 103rd Congress compared to just 37 percent of Republican men. However, in the 104th Congress, the percentage of Republican women sponsoring women's issue bills fell dramatically. This 24 percent drop in the percentage of Republican women sponsoring women's issue bills is largely due to the election of six conservative Republican freshman women, none of whom sponsored any type of women's issue bill, feminist, traditional, or antifeminist. By contrast, only one of the ten Republican women who served in both the 103rd and 104th Congresses reduced her sponsorship of women's issue bills to zero. The other nine women reacted to their new majority status by maintaining the same level of sponsorship or by increasing their sponsorship.

At first glance, the lack of interest in women's issue bills displayed by these new conservative Republican women might be attributed to their freshman status. Freshman legislators must spend time solidifying their hold on their districts and building their reelection constituencies, leading many to focus on specific district concerns (Fenno 1978). Thus, Barbara Cubin (R-WY) and Helen Chenoweth (R-ID), both from western districts with large amounts of public land, concentrated their attention on reducing environmental regulations. However, a comparison of women's issue bill sponsorship by equally conservative Republican men does not reveal any important differences between freshman and nonfreshman since 46 percent of the conservative freshman and 41 percent of their more senior conservative counterparts sponsored women's issue bills.[6] This finding provides tentative evidence that conservative women are no more likely to make women's issues a priority than are their male conservative colleagues, and they may, in fact, actually be less interested in these issues.

Comparing Gender Differences by Policy Area

Table 3 reveals important gender differences in the type of legislator who sponsors feminist, social welfare, and antifeminist bills. Across both the 103rd and 104th Congresses, Democratic and Republican men are more likely to sponsor a social welfare bill than a feminist bill. Since many of the social welfare bills concern core issues like health care and education that generate high levels of interest among voters, many legislators responded to constituent concerns about health care by sponsoring bills to make health insurance costs tax deductible for the self-employed, to expand patients' rights, or to guarantee health insurance portability. As rational choice theories of congressional behavior (Mayhew 1974; Arnold 1990) would predict, these bills allowed them to claim credit for taking a position and avoid blame for congressional inaction on health issues.

Moreover, within the institution of Congress, social welfare policies are highly integrated into committee jurisdictions and the reauthorization process, and they are a major component of the issues that have divided the parties since the New Deal (Burnham 1970). Thus, as a group, Democratic and Republican congressmen who offered social welfare proposals responded to the dual motivations of constituency demand and institutional responsibilities.

In contrast, feminist issues like abortion, sexual harassment, and gender equity in education do not provide ideal opportunities for credit claiming since their benefits are diffuse and cannot be directly targeted at the district the way increased funding for local schools can. Furthermore, these feminist issues are often controversial. They have the potential to expose cleavages within a member's political party and to mobilize the grassroots organizations of powerful interest groups into opposition in the next election. Therefore, rational legislators will avoid expending political capital on developing feminist legislation and will limit themselves to establishing a voting record that reflects the feelings of the majority in their district. Indeed, by devoting more resources to the pursuit of social welfare legislation rather than feminist legislation, as a group, congressmen's sponsorship behavior conforms to the predictions of rational choice theory.

In contrast to Democratic and Republican men, the behavior of congresswomen does not conform to the picture of the rational legislator who avoids sponsoring controversial feminist legislation in favor of proposals concerning social welfare issues. Congresswomen of both parties, particularly in the 103rd Congress, sponsored more feminist legislation than social welfare initiatives. The pattern is most striking among Republican women, as the small group of twelve Republican women sponsored more feminist bills than their 163 Republican male counterparts. Thus, it appears that gender provided the added intensity of interest to make feminist bills a priority and to encourage Democratic and Republican congresswomen to risk exposing partisan cleavages and mobilizing opposition interest groups to place feminist issues on the national agenda.

During the 104th Congress, Democratic women continued to sponsor more feminist bills than social welfare bills. In fact, Democratic women offered almost as many feminist proposals as did their more numerous Republican and Democratic male colleagues combined. However, in the 104th Congress, Republican women reversed their sponsorship patterns and proposed more bills concerning social welfare issues than feminist issues. It is possible that Republican women shifted their resources to social welfare legislation because, as members of the majority party, they now had more opportunities to see their preferences on these issues passed into law. At the same time, they may have focused their attention on social welfare initiatives because feminist proposals would create conflict with conservative Republican Party caucus members and key Republican interest group supporters such as conservative Christians. For example, a staff member for a moderate Republican woman noted that since she arrived in the 103rd Congress, her congresswoman has sponsored a bill to provide tax credits to employers who offer child-care services for their employees. However, she has largely given up on building support for this bill because liberals do not want to give tax breaks to businesses and the social conservatives in her party are opposed to child-care legislation. Clearly, the congresswoman recognizes that members who expose conflicts within the party and antagonize important supporters invite sanctions from party leaders, which would prevent them from seeing their priorities passed in other policy and constituency-related areas. Therefore, moderate Republican women needed to guard their political capital and professional reputation by balancing their abstract policy preferences against what their fellow party members would support.

Finally, as demonstrated in table 3, Republican men sponsor the overwhelming majority of antifeminist bills. Thus, when agenda control shifted to the Republicans in the 104th Congress, the number of antifeminist bills offered by Republican congressmen more than tripled, rising from thirteen to forty bills. The rise in antifeminist proposals reflects both the increasingly conservative Republican membership and the status of social conservatives as a key Republican constituency. Groups such as the Christian Coalition, Concerned Women for America, and the Family Research Council expected the new Republican majority to reverse policies implemented by the Clinton Administration and the Democratic majority, which were passed with support from liberal feminist groups.

Among Republican women, none of the new conservative freshmen sponsored an antifeminist bill or any other women's issue bill, while 19 percent of the thirty-six conservative male Republican freshmen sponsored antifeminist bills. However, as shown in chapter 4, these women were active cosponsors of antifeminist legislation, with all but one cosponsoring more than the Republican average of five antifeminist bills. Additionally, in media interviews, these women made a point of stating that they did not "claim sisterhood with the so-called 'women's agenda'" and that they viewed themselves as "citizens" rather than as women (Miller 1995). As these conservative women gain seniority and as more conservative women are elected, it is an open question as to whether they will continue to ignore women's issues and insist that they do not exist or whether they will actively engage these issues from a conservative or antifeminist viewpoint.

The two Republican women who sponsored antifeminist bills, Barbara Vucanovich (R-NV) and Jan Meyers (R-KS), both held leadership positions in the 104th Congress. Vucanovich served as conference secretary and sponsored a plank of the Contract with America that included provisions concerning parental rights, which would require parental permission for children to be involved in surveys.[7] As chair of the Small Business Committee, Meyers sponsored a compromise antiaffirmative action bill that Republicans supported after a more sweeping bill by Constitution Subcommittee chair, Charles Canady, failed (Clemmitt, Primmer, and Simms 1997). The sponsorship patterns of these two Republican women raise important questions of how women will behave when they reach positions of power in party leadership and on committees, in particular how they will respond to party goals and whether they will make women's issues a priority from either a feminist or antifeminist point of view.

Modeling Gender Effects on Women's Issue Bill Sponsorship

While the results in tables 2 and 3 indicate that there are important gender differences in the willingness of representatives to support women's issue legislation, it is possible that these findings do not reflect the unique policy contributions of women but could be better explained by other factors. For example, what appears to be a gender effect may really reflect the fact that more women are being elected from very liberal districts, therefore all liberal Democrats will make gender-related legislation a priority. Alternatively, it is possible that women are more active advocates for women's issue initiatives because they are more likely to serve on committees that deal with these issues, and therefore any perceived gender dynamics actually are a function of members carrying out their committee responsibilities. To determine whether the gender differences in legislators' women's issue bill sponsorship patterns persist after one accounts for the other personal, partisan, constituency, and institutional factors that influence the policy priorities of members, I rely on multivariate ordered logit analysis.

The ordered logit models in tables 4 and 5 allow me to test the importance of gender as an indicator of which members will pursue women's initiatives while taking into account other important influences on congressional behavior. In table 4, the dependent variables measure whether each member sponsored 0, 1, or 2 or more women's issue bills.[8] Similarly, in table 5 the dependent variables account for the number of feminist and social welfare issue bills proposed by each representative.[9] Too few legislators sponsored antifeminist bills to warrant a separate regression analysis.

The independent variables employed in the regression analyses in tables 4 and 5 and throughout the book draw on the vast congressional research concerning the elements that motivate legislators' policy decisions. Since party affiliation is one of the most reliable guides to how members of Congress approach issues (Rhode 1991; Cox and

Table 4 Ordered Logits on Women's Issue Bills

Independent Variables	All Women's Issue Bills	
	103rd Congress	104th Congress
Republican women	2.13**	1.8*
	(2.73)	(2.25)
Democratic women	1.64***	1.41***
	(3.92)	(3.31)
Republican men	.187	.748
	(.33)	(1.16)
Ideology	−.104	−1.04
	(−.15)	(−1.61)
Religion	−.371	.193
	(−1.54)	(.86)
Freshman	−.275	−.474
	(−1.01)	(−1.63)
% Vote for Clinton	3.17+	.53
	(1.78)	(.28)
% Vote for Perot	.683	−2.94
	(.27)	(−1.13)
% Urban	1.54*	.634
	(2.39)	(1.04)
% Black	−1.31	−1.18
	(−1.26)	(−1.2)
Median household income	.108	.138
	(.68)	(.85)
Woman's subcommittee	.804**	.754***
	(3.08)	(3.18)
Woman's subcommittee chair	−.389	2.28+
	(−.44)	(1.95)
Woman's committee chair	1.69	1.47
	(1.63)	(1.34)
No. of bills	.1***	.111***
	(6.98)	(7.12)
Number of observations	432	429
% Correct	64	59
PRE statistic (%)	19	15
PRE ± 1 (%)	41	36

NOTE: Numbers in parentheses are *Z*-statistics (coefficient/standard errors).
+*p* ≤ .1.
* *p* ≤ .05.
** *p* ≤ .01.
*** *p* ≤ .001.

Table 5 Ordered Logits on Feminist and Social Welfare Bill Sponsorship

Independent Variables	103rd Congress		104th Congress	
	Feminist	Social Welfare	Feminist	Social Welfare
Republican women	3.27***	.323	5.08***	1.38+
	(3.56)	(.41)	(4.37)	(1.72)
Democratic women	1.78***	1.19**	2.32***	.82*
	(4.06)	(2.88)	(4.96)	(1.96)
Republican men	.332	−.129	3.25**	.147
	(.41)	(−.21)	(3.05)	(.22)
Ideology	−.962	.315	−4.37***	−.322
	(−1.04)	(.44)	(−4.21)	(−.48)
Freshman	.129	−.77*	−.435	−.429
	(.35)	(−2.45)	(.82)	(−1.38)
Hispanic representative	.078	1.33*	−.778	.955
	(.11)	(2.23)	(−.92)	(1.63)
Religion	−.517	−.597*	−.17	−.032
	(−1.61)	(−2.18)	(−.05)	(−.38)
Southern	−.642	−.156	.486	.005
	(−1.57)	(−.5)	(1.11)	(.02)
% Vote for Clinton	2.36	2.61	−4.25+	3.62*
	(1.05)	(1.4)	(−1.72)	(2)
% Urban	1.84*	.591	2.98**	−.672
	(2.04)	(.83)	(2.9)	(−1.01)
% Black	−2.76+	.161	−.464	−1.57
	(−1.91)	(.14)	(−.32)	(−1.41)
Median household income	−.067	.385*	.003	.259
	(−.3)	(2.13)	(.01)	(1.46)
Feminist/social welfare subcommittee	.529	.65*	.612	.649*
	(1.56)	(2.48)	(1.61)	(2.44)
Feminist/social welfare subcommittee chair	−.825	. . .	−.397	2.57*
	(−.88)		(−.37)	(2.23)
Feminist/social welfare subcommittee ranking member	−.203	. . .	−1.81	1.4
	(−.18)		(−1.35)	(1.4)
Woman's committee chair	.527	2.59*	−.654	2.51*
	(.82)	(2.21)	(−.52)	(2.09)
Woman's committee ranking member	.79	. . .	.373	1.01
	(1.01)		(.51)	(1.54)
No. of bills	.099***	.062***	.124***	.091***
	(6.6)	(5.08)	(7.34)	(6.19)
Number of observations	432	432	429	429
% Correct	81	71	85	63
PRE statistic (%)	16	10	22	9
PRE ±1 (%)	35	27	38	30

NOTE: Numbers in parentheses are Z-statistics (coefficient/standard errors).
+ $p \leq .1$.
* $p \leq .05$.
** $p \leq .01$.
*** $p \leq .001$.

McCubbins 1993; Aldrich 1995), I created variables for Republican men and women and Democratic men and women. Dividing men and women by party allows me to examine the ways in which partisanship affects a member's willingness to pursue preferences based on gender. The models in tables 4 and 5 and throughout the book include the dummy variables measuring Democratic women and Republican men and women. Since one would expect Democrats to be the most supportive of women's issue proposals, Democratic men are always the "out category" and therefore the comparison category. Thus, a positive and significant coefficient for Democratic women would indicate that being a Democratic woman has an important influence on the decision to sponsor a women's issue bill and Democratic women are even more likely to sponsor these bills than are Democratic men.

To capture intraparty differences on women's issues, I rely on Poole-Rosenthal DW-NOMINATE scores as a measure of individual ideology (Poole and Rosenthal 1997). These scores range from -1, indicating most liberal, to $+1$, indicating most conservative. Thus, an expected negative relationship between the ideology score and support for women's issue legislation would indicate that these issues tend to be supported by the most liberal members within the party caucus.[10]

Since the needs of the district rank foremost in the minds of all representatives (Fiorina 1974; Mayhew 1974; Fenno 1978; Arnold 1990), I account for the characteristics of the legislator's constituency by including census data measuring the percentage of the district that is urban, the district's median household income, the percentage of African-Americans in the district, the percentage of Hispanics in the district, and whether the district is in a Southern state.[11] Additional variables measuring the percentage of the district voting for Clinton and for Perot in the 1992 election are used to assess how democratic the district is and the level of independence within the district. I also incorporated variables that measure personal characteristics beyond gender, including the race and religion of the representative.[12]

Finally, any effort to discern how members determine their legislative priorities must consider the individual legislator's status within the institution. Therefore, I include variables for freshman status and committee position. Committee scholars note that representatives who sit on relevant committees and subcommittees gain important advantages in their areas of jurisdiction, including access to expert staff to help draft legislation and gatekeeping authority to block or advance proposals. The committee and subcommittee leaders enjoy even more policy advantages than do individual committee members (Shepsle and

Weingast 1987; Krehbiel 1991; Norton 1994, 2002; Hall 1996). While committee position is essential to a legislator's ability to play an active role in shaping policy, women's issues do not fall within clear committee jurisdictions. Therefore, I developed variables that incorporate the committees and subcommittees that considered the most women's issue legislation and the chairs and ranking minority members of these bodies.[13] Also, a variable measuring the total number of bills each member sponsored accounts for the fact that those who sponsor more bills are mathematically more likely to sponsor a women's issue bill.

Understanding How Gender Influences Policy

The results in tables 4 and 5 demonstrate that gender has a highly significant impact on a representative's decision to sponsor women's issue bills, and gender exerts an even more important effect on the decision to propose feminist bills. As predicted, the impact of being a female representative is secondary to other constituency factors and to committee position in terms of the decision to sponsor social welfare bills.[14]

The fact that a legislator is a Democratic woman is a consistently large and significant determinant of which representatives sponsor the full set of women's issue bills and the subset of feminist legislation, even after one takes into account their liberal ideology and the level of Democratic support in their districts (as measured by the percentage of the district that voted for President Clinton in the 1992 election).

Similarly, across both Congresses, the large and significant coefficients for Republican women demonstrate that these women consistently defected from their party's traditional position on women's issues, particularly feminist issues. In fact, being a Republican woman exerted a more important influence on sponsorship of feminist legislation than any other variable including constituency characteristics, ideology, or committee position.

It may appear surprising that being a Republican man, while generally insignificant, exerts a positive impact on women's issue bill sponsorship. However, the inclusion of variables accounting for ideology and the district vote for Clinton allows the Republican male coefficient to highlight the influence of moderate Republican men from more Democratic districts. For example, if the feminist bill sponsorship model for the 104th Congress excludes the ideology variable, Republican women remain a positive and significant predictor of which members sponsor feminist bills, while being a Republican man exerts a negative and significant impact on a member's decision to initiate feminist legislation.[15]

With regard to social welfare legislation, the importance of gender depends on which party controls the House. In the Democratically controlled 103rd Congress, being a Democratic woman is a significant predictor of which members propose social welfare bills, while in the Republican 104th Congress, Republican women are among the most active sponsors of social welfare initiatives. Since the majority party maintains responsibility and control over the agenda on social welfare issues, as members of the majority party, women recognize the increased potential that their proposals will be incorporated into law, and they are even more motivated to spend time on these issues than are their male partisan colleagues. The influence of majority party status on women's sponsorship behavior supports the findings of scholars who maintain that legislative outcomes reflect the preferences of the median voter in the majority party caucus (Rhode 1991; Cox and McCubbins 1993; Aldrich and Rhode 1995, 1997, 2000) rather than the median voter on the House floor (Krehbiel 1991, 1998).

While gender is among the most significant, if not the most important, influence on feminist bill sponsorship, gender plays a secondary role to other personal, constituency, and institutional factors in determining sponsorship of social welfare bills. For example, Hispanic representatives are almost as likely to sponsor social welfare initiatives as the women of the majority party are. However, being a Hispanic representative has no impact on the decision to sponsor feminist bills. Furthermore, the significance of majority party women appears to come from the tendency of these women to sponsor more than one bill in these areas. When logit models (models not shown) are run simply to determine whether a legislator sponsors a social welfare bill, being a majority party woman is not a significant influence on the sponsorship decision.

Among the district variables, the percentage of the district voting for Clinton is a consistently larger and more important determinant of activity on social welfare issues than gender is. It makes sense that representatives from highly Democratic districts will sponsor more social welfare legislation because these issues tend to be associated with the Democratic Party.[16] The public, particularly women, favors Democrats on these "compassion" issues. President Clinton benefited from a gender gap in the 1992 elections, and that gap grew even wider in the 1996 elections. The fact that the Clinton vote coefficient is a consistently insignificant determinant of which members sponsor feminist bills indicates that representatives prefer to propose legislation that is less ideologically charged and does not divide their constituencies.

Finally, institutional clout as measured by committee position exerts an important influence on which members will sponsor social welfare bills. While committee and subcommittee position has little impact on a member's decision to sponsor feminist legislation, a seat on a relevant subcommittee is a consistently significant predictor of activity on social welfare issues.[17] Similarly, in his analysis of legislative participation in committees, Hall (1996) found that subcommittee members participated more in committee deliberations on specific bills than did their counterparts on the full committee.

Moreover, the regression results demonstrate that committee leaders, particularly woman's committee chairs and social welfare subcommittee chairs, exercise important advantages of responsibility for and power over social welfare issues that allow them to be more active participants in policy making on these issues. The fact that committee leadership is not an important indicator of feminist bill sponsorship demonstrates that feminist legislation provides an opportunity for some less senior members, particularly women, to carve a policy niche for themselves and bring new issues and ideas to the congressional agenda. It also indicates that feminist issues might gain more attention from the committees if more women ascend to leadership positions.

What If There Were More Women in Congress?

To get a more precise picture of how much gender influences the likelihood that a member will sponsor a women's issue bill, I calculated predicted probabilities for Republican and Democratic men and women. Predicted probabilities allow one to determine how likely it is that an event will occur given certain conditions, in this case the gender, party affiliation, ideological stance, and level of Democratic support in a member's district, as measured by the district vote for Bill Clinton in 1992. Predicted probabilities do not deal with actual members. Instead, they allow one to create hypothetical members and to assign them specific characteristics such as a conservative ideology or a high level of Democratic support in their districts. Using predicted probabilities, I can predict what would likely occur if more women were elected to the House.

For example, in figure 3, the first bar indicates that, in the 103rd Congress, a conservative Democratic man who represents a district that registered a lower vote for Bill Clinton than other districts represented

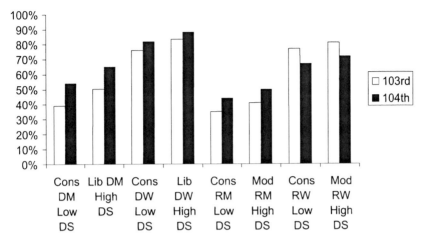

Figure 3   Probability of Sponsoring a Women's Issue Bill

NOTE: *Cons* = conservative; *Lib* = liberal; *Mod* = moderate; *DM* = Democratic men; *DW* = Democratic women; *RM* = Republican men; *RW* = Republican women; *Low DS* = low-level of Democratic support in the district; and *High DS* = high-level of Democratic support in the district. The bars represent the mean probability that a member with a given gender, party, ideology, and level of Democratic support in the district, as measured by the district vote for Bill Clinton in 1992, will sponsor a women's issue bill. To characterize members as hypothetical liberal or conservative Democrats and moderate or conservative Republicans, the ideology scores are set at the 25 percent and 75 percent quartiles within each party. Similarly, members are assigned a high or low level of district support for Democrats by setting the vote for Clinton at the 25 percent and 75 percent quartile levels within each party.

by Democrats will exhibit, on average, a 39 percent chance of sponsoring a women's issue bill.[18] Similarly, the last bar in figure 4 indicates that, in the 104th Congress, a moderate Republican woman who represents a district that registered a higher vote for Bill Clinton than other districts represented by Republicans will exhibit, on average, a 32 percent chance of sponsoring a feminist bill. Since the ordered logit models in table 5 demonstrate that ideology was not an important determinant of which members sponsor social welfare bills, figure 5 measures the likelihood that a member with a given gender, party affiliation, and level of Democratic support in the district will sponsor a social welfare bill.

Figure 3 demonstrates that in both the 103rd and the 104th Congresses, women of all ideological persuasions and district types are more likely to sponsor women's issue bills than are their male colleagues. The largest differences occur on the more controversial feminist legislation (see fig. 4). For example, in the 103rd Congress, liberal Democratic

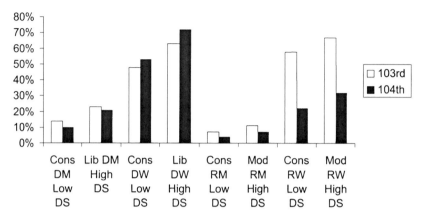

Figure 4 Probability of Sponsoring a Feminist Bill

NOTE: *Cons* = conservative; *Lib* = liberal; *Mod* = moderate; *DM* = Democratic men; *DW* = Democratic women; *RM* = Republican men; *RW* = Republican women; *Low DS* = low-level of Democratic support in the district; and *High DS* = high-level of Democratic support in the district. The bars represent the mean probability that a member with a given gender, party, ideology, and level of Democratic support in the district, as measured by the district vote for Bill Clinton in 1992, will sponsor a feminist issue bill. To characterize members as hypothetical liberal or conservative Democrats and moderate or conservative Republicans, the ideology scores are set at the 25 percent and 75 percent quartiles within each party. Similarly, members are assigned a high or low level of district support for Democrats by setting the vote for Clinton at the 25 percent and 75 percent quartile levels within each party.

women were 40 percent more likely than liberal Democratic men, and moderate Republican women were more than 55 percent more likely than moderate Republican men, to sponsor a feminist bill. With regard to social welfare legislation, this gap is reduced. The difference in the probability that a Democratic woman will sponsor more social welfare bills than a similarly situated Democratic man is less than 30 percent in the 103rd Congress and less than 20 percent in the 104th Congress. Similarly, Republican women were only about 10 percent more likely than were their male colleagues to sponsor a social welfare bill in the 103rd Congress and these women were 28 percent more likely than were Republican men to initiate these bills in the 104th Congress.

Across both Congresses, the probability that a Democratic woman will sponsor a women's issue bill is over 50 percent in all policy areas. In contrast, the pattern of women's issue bill sponsorship among Republican women changed dramatically between the 103rd and 104th Congresses. The probability that a moderate or conservative Republican woman would sponsor a feminist bill dropped almost forty percentage points between the two Congresses, resulting in less than a 30 percent

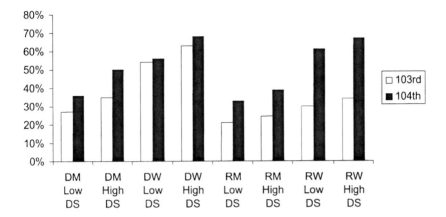

Figure 5 Probability of Sponsoring a Social Welfare Bill

NOTE: *DM* = Democratic men; *DW* = Democratic women; *RM* = Republican men; *RW* = Republican women; *Low DS* = low-level of Democratic support in the district; and *High DS* = high-level of Democratic support in the district. The bars represent the mean probability that a member with a given gender, party, and level of Democratic support in the district, as measured by the district vote for Bill Clinton in 1992, will sponsor a social welfare bill. Members are assigned a high or low level of district support for Democrats by setting the vote for Clinton at the 25 percent and 75 percent quartile levels within each party.

chance that a Republican woman in the 104th Congress would sponsor a feminist bill. Yet, the probability that a Republican woman would propose a social welfare bill increased to over 60 percent between the 103rd and the 104th Congresses.

The shift in the behavior of Republican women highlights the influence of the political and institutional contexts on members' legislative decisions. When Republican women were in the minority they were more willing to defect from their party's traditional position on feminist legislation. The ascendancy of Republicans to the majority increased the opportunities for Republican women to see legislative action on their priorities on a wide range of issues. However, majority status also gave the Republican leadership access to stronger sanctions to punish members who acted against the preferences of the majority of the party caucus and core Republican constituencies, such as the social conservatives. Additionally, the 104th Congress was much more ideologically polarized than the 103rd, which increased partisan conflict and the importance placed on party loyalty. The combination of a politically polarized Congress and the prerogatives of majority status led Republican women to eschew controversial feminist initiatives that would divide the caucus and to utilize their new majority status to influence the direction of social welfare policies.

Indeed, in their study of welfare reform, Casey and Carroll (1998) found that moderate Republican women like Nancy Johnson (R-CT), who was a senior member of the committee with jurisdiction over welfare reform, had to pick their battles with Republican leaders carefully in order to moderate the welfare reform bill with respect to issues such as the expansion of child-support enforcement and an increase in funding for child care. In interviews, some moderate Republican members asserted that it is difficult to advocate for feminist issues like family planning and child care because "you do not want to be perceived as an advocate for Democratic interest groups." This perception damages one's credibility within the party conference. Thus, when moderate Republican women take on feminist issues, they must work against fellow party members, their natural allies. This situation compounds the inherent difficulty of moving an issue onto the national agenda. Therefore, in the 104th Congress, Republican women appear to have adjusted their legislative goals on women's issues to proposals that fit more easily within the Republican agenda.

Translating Interest into Action: Whose Bills Become Law?

While congresswomen may exhibit a greater interest in women's issue legislation, interest does not guarantee action. A closer inspection of whose bills became law or were incorporated into bills that became law highlights the extreme importance of committee position. The structure of the committee system gives committee members an incentive to develop expertise in the areas under their jurisdiction. Committee members, particularly subcommittee members, are given the responsibility to draft proposals, and they generally manage debate on the floor and have the final word in conference committees. Furthermore, subcommittee and committee chairs decide when bills will be scheduled for markup and generally control the specifics included in the final bill (Shepsle and Weingast 1987; Smith and Deering 1990; Krehbiel 1991).

Forty-nine of the ninety bills that saw some action in the 103rd Congress and thirty-seven of the eighty-seven bills with action in the 104th Congress became law either as free-standing bills or through incorporation into other bills. Of these eighty-six bills, 70 percent (sixty bills) were sponsored by the committee or subcommittee chair with jurisdiction over the bill, and three more bills were sponsored by ranking minority members. Eleven more of the bills that became law were offered by members of the committee or subcommittee with jurisdiction over the bill, and three bills were sponsored by party leaders. Members who were not on the committee with jurisdiction initiated only ten bills, or 12 percent of the bills that became law: seven in the 103rd Congress and three in the 104th Congress.

In the 103rd Congress, women sponsored five of the seven bills that were initiated by a non–committee member. However, in the 104th Congress, only three women, Susan Molinari (R-NY), Barbara Vucanovich (R-NV), and Nancy Johnson (R-CT), saw their women's issue bills enacted into law. Susan Molinari and Barbara Vucanovich were members of the Republican Party leadership as conference vice-chair and secretary, respectively. Nancy Johnson was a member of the powerful Ways and Means Committee and chaired its Oversight Subcommittee. Thus, in the 104th Congress, only women with positions of power could influence the legislative agenda on women's issues.

It is clear that regardless of one's level of interest in women's issue bills, committee and subcommittee leaders are the gatekeepers of what issues get placed on the national agenda. Given the important role gender plays in determining interest in women's issues, the appointment of more women to relevant committee and subcommittee chairs could increase the openness of the congressional agenda to women's issue legislation. However, institutional influence is tempered by partisan context. The committee chairs in the 103rd Congress had more independence from party leaders than did committee chairs in the 104th Congress, and the agenda of the Republican majority was much less open to liberal proposals on women's issues. Thus, congresswomen who gain leadership posts in the committees will have more freedom to pursue preferences based on gender, but that freedom will still be constrained by their party's agenda and the willingness of the party leadership to bring their bills to the floor for a vote.

Conclusion

The analysis of gender differences in bill sponsorship for the 103rd and 104th Congresses provides evidence that congresswomen exhibit greater interest in the pursuit and advocacy of women's issue legislation than do their male colleagues. Women are utilizing their scarce political capital and staff resources to shine a spotlight on women's issues, particularly feminist issues such as domestic violence, reproductive rights, and child care.

The changes in women's sponsorship patterns across the 103rd and 104th Congresses demonstrate that congresswomen, like all legislators, adjust their policy goals to the realities of the political and institutional context. Representatives choose their policy priorities with an eye toward what their district constituency and fellow party members will accept as well as an assessment of their position within the committee structure and the larger institution. Thus, both Democratic and Republican congresswomen focused more of their attention on social welfare bills when their party held the majority, and they therefore could exercise greater influence over the direction of policy on these issues. Similarly, moderate Republican women may have shifted their resources away from feminist issues in the 104th Congress because they recognized that they risked losing opportunities to see action on other policy priorities if they antagonized party leaders, fellow Republican caucus members, and key social conservative interest groups.

Finally, the review of which legislators' bills become law demonstrates that committee and subcommittee members, especially the committee and subcommittee leaders, exercise tremendous influence over which initiatives receive attention. Regardless of one's interest in women's issues, without a seat at the policy-making table, a legislator will find it very difficult to influence the agenda.

Chapter 4

Cosponsorship:
Registering Support for Women's Issues

Every day members of Congress receive a stack of "Dear Colleague" letters from their fellow representatives asking them to demonstrate support for an issue by cosponsoring their bill. On any given day, a legislator can sign on to a bill that promises to preserve the budget surplus for saving Social Security and paying down the debt while, at the same time, he or she can cosponsor bills that will increase funding for education, provide prescription drug coverage for seniors, and place a moratorium on the taxation of Internet commerce. Clearly, cosponsorship allows members to take positions on a wide range of issues with relatively little effort. All representatives, whether they are a member of the committee of jurisdiction or a freshman minority party member with limited influence over the policy-making process, can cosponsor a bill. Thus, cosponsorship can be described as loud voting because legislators are not forced to take a position as they are with a roll-call vote but they can choose to register their views on an issue by signing their names as cosponsors.

Thus, analyzing the number of women's issue bills that representatives cosponsor indicates which representatives have a general interest in women's issues, although it cannot reveal the depth of members' commitment to women's issues. This chapter evaluates whether gender is an important predictor of interest in the wide range of women's issue legislation, once one accounts for the partisan, constituency, and institutional factors that influence members' cosponsorship decisions. The examination of gender differences in cosponsorship provides more evidence that the election of more women to Congress could make the national policy agenda more open to gender-related legislation.

Why Do Members Cosponsor?

Research demonstrates that cosponsorship serves two main purposes: it facilitates members' electoral goals by allowing them to take a position on an issue and it acts as an internal legislative signal informing members about the content of legislation and the level of support for a bill (Krehbiel 1995; Kessler and Krehbiel 1996; Wilson and Young 1997; Balla and Nemacheck 1999). On the electoral side, by cosponsoring a bill, members can advertise positions on issues favored by important segments of their constituencies without necessarily caring about the ultimate fate of a bill. For example, according to a conservative Democratic congressman, there is a group of about forty pro-life Democrats that actively look for opportunities to sponsor or cosponsor bills that are friendly to women and children to compensate for their pro-life position within both their districts and the Democratic Party caucus.

The idea that cosponsorship is a quick and inexpensive way to advertise positions is reinforced by the fact that members cosponsor so many bills and often have very loose criteria for determining which bills to cosponsor. In addition, while some members must approve any action taken by the office, cosponsorship is often a staff-driven process in which staffers use their knowledge of the member's preferences to determine whether to sign onto a bill. Representatives cosponsored an average of 267 bills in the 103rd Congress and 171 bills in the 104th Congress. In the 103rd Congress, cosponsorship rates ranged from a low of fourteen bills cosponsored by Ways and Means chair Dan Rostenkowski (D-IL) to a high of 757 bills cosponsored by Martin Frost (D-TX), while in the 104th Congress, the number of bills cosponsored ranged from a low of seventeen bills by freshman Lloyd Doggett (D-TX) to a high of 492 bills by William Lipinski (D-IL). When interviewed, members and staff pointed to a few very general criteria for determining which bills to cosponsor. For example, one staffer said that her representative will cosponsor a bill if "she supports an idea or if she gets a request from constituents. She will also cosponsor bills if constituents or [interest] groups ask what she is doing on an issue because then she can say she cosponsored a bill on it." Another staffer said that since her representative is a fiscal conservative, she cosponsors bills if "she believes in the idea and it does not cost the government money or it has an offset for the costs." Other members use a basic ideological criterion. A conservative Democrat said that he will cosponsor a bill if he sees that the other cosponsors agree with him philosophically but he will move more to the left if the sponsor is a friend. Similarly, another staffer said that she looks at who else is cosponsoring the legislation to get an idea of the ideological bent of the bill. If "a lot of left-wingers" are cosponsoring, then her representative won't cosponsor the bill.

Beyond electoral considerations, cosponsorship also acts as an internal legislative signal, transmitting information about the content of a bill and the degree of support within the institution. For example, Kessler and Krehbiel (1996) found that where extremists from both sides of the policy spectrum cosponsor legislation in the early stages of a bill's cycle, moderates will sign on at later stages. They conclude that these "heterogeneous extremists" are policy experts sending out confirmatory signals that the potential policy consequences of the legislation will conform to those outcomes favored by a congressional majority.

In interviews, most members and staff referred to cosponsorship as an important aspect of coalition building. Many expressed a desire to find a lead cosponsor in the opposition party in order to demonstrate that their bill has bipartisan support. Others claimed that a legislator needs more cosponsors if one is not on the committee of jurisdiction or if he or she does not have the support of the committee chair. For example, a Democratic congresswoman who was trying to get support for a bill concerning gender equity in education explained that the Republican committee and subcommittee chairs did not support her bill. Therefore, she planned to send Dear Colleague letters, have her staff call members' offices, and lobby members on the floor in an effort to get enough Republican members to support the bill to be able to defeat the committee leaders. Furthermore, members and staff believe that getting more cosponsors on a bill increases its chance of passage on the floor. One staffer explained, "You want a lot of cosponsors on your bill because they are seen as secure votes, people who endorse the bill, and the fact that a certain person is a cosponsor will influence how others vote." Although members and the media tout the number of cosponsors on a bill as a predictor of passage, Wilson and Young (1997) found that bills with more cosponsors are more likely to gain committee consideration but that the number of cosponsors has no impact on whether a bill will be considered on the floor.

While much of the research on cosponsorship has centered on the impact of cosponsorship on bill passage and the status of cosponsorship as an electoral tool or an internal legislative signal, few studies have examined the characteristics of members who cosponsor bills in specific policy areas. With regard to race, Canon (1999) found that African-American representatives were much more likely to sponsor and cosponsor legislation with racial content than were white representatives with large minority populations in their districts. Balla and Nemacheck's (1999) study of cosponsorship of managed-care legislation in the 105th Congress provides preliminary support for the notion that congresswomen will be more supportive of women's issue legislation. These researchers found that gender was a significant predictor of cosponsorship on targeted bills, many of which addressed women's health concerns, but gender did not have an impact on the decision to cosponsor comprehensive managed-care reform bills. Similarly, Wolbrecht (2000, 2002) found that, over the forty-year period from 1953 to 1992, congresswomen were more likely to cosponsor legislation concerning women's rights and that female legislators played an active role in bringing new women's rights proposals to the congressional agenda. In this chapter, I examine whether their common social identity leads congresswomen to actively promote attention to women's interests by signing on to gender-related legislation.

Uncovering Gender Effects on Cosponsorship

To gauge members' cosponsorship activity on women's issues, I coded the number of representatives cosponsoring each of the 510 women's issue bills in the 103rd Congress and the 569 bills in the 104th Congress. The number of cosponsors on a bill can range from zero to almost an entire party delegation when a bill reflects an issue of contention between the two parties. For example, in the 103rd Congress, the Clinton Health Plan and the Republican alternative had 103 Democratic and 140 Republican cosponsors, respectively, while in the 104th Congress, the Republican Welfare Reform Bill had 119 Republican cosponsors. I then developed a score that measures the number of women's issue bills cosponsored by each representative. During the two Congresses, representatives signed their names to a minimum of one and a maximum of 114 bills in the 103rd Congress and 115 bills in the 104th Congress.[1]

Table 6 provides a first look at women's issue bill cosponsorship patterns in the 103rd and 104th Congresses. Since members and staff repeatedly cited the ideological views of other cosponsors as an important determinant of their decision to cosponsor a bill, the data are divided by gender, party, and ideology. The table displays the mean number of women's issue bills cosponsored and the standard deviation for liberal and conservative Democratic and moderate and conservative Republican men and women.[2]

The most dramatic gender difference highlighted by the table is in the policy focus of the social liberals within each party. Liberal Democratic

Table 6 The 103rd and 104th Congresses: Means for All Women's Issue Bill Cosponsorship

	Democrat				Republican			
	Men		Women		Men		Women	
Congress	Conservative	Liberal	Conservative	Liberal	Conservative	Moderate	Conservative	Moderate
103rd	17	33	36	52	17	21	22	36
	(13)	(22)	(21)	(21)	(7.5)	(11)	(5)	(21)
104th	18	33	27	49	23	25	27	38
	(12)	(20)	(13)	(19)	(11)	(13)	(7)	(13)
No. of representatives:								
103rd	72	150	5	30	119	44	4	8
104th	54	111	4	26	156	61	9	8

NOTE: Standard deviations are in parentheses.

women cosponsored the largest number of women's issue bills in both Congresses. In the 103rd Congress, the mean number of women's issue bills cosponsored by liberal Democratic women is nineteen more than the mean for liberal Democratic men. In the 104th Congress, the difference of means between liberal Democratic men and women is sixteen bills. Similarly, among Republicans, the difference in the mean number of bills cosponsored is largest between moderate Republican men and women. This finding demonstrates that liberal Democratic men and women may vote similarly on the floor but that liberal Democratic women will be more interested in placing women's issues on the national agenda. This statement also holds true for moderate Republican men and women. Furthermore, conservative women within both parties cosponsor women's issue bills at rates that are equivalent to their more moderate and liberal male partisan counterparts.

A focus on the changing patterns of cosponsorship between the 103rd and 104th Congresses reveals that conservative Republican men and women registered the largest increases in women's issue bill cosponsorship while the average number of women's issue bills cosponsored by conservative and liberal Democratic women declined. This pattern is consistent with the idea that after Republicans won the majority, the conservatives took control of the policy agenda and congresswomen, who were mostly Democrats, lost influence over the direction of policy on women's issues. As one staffer for a liberal Democratic congressman said: "When you are in the majority, 90 percent of what you do is to do good and make policy. In the minority, 90 percent of what you do is to try to stop bad things from happening. It is frustrating. The majority controls what bills come up and what you are going to have hearings on. That is why we now have the Defense of Marriage Act instead of the Employment Non-Discrimination Act and crime bills that emphasize the Ten Commandments instead of midnight basketball."[3]

As with bill sponsorship, when the cosponsorship data are divided by policy area and direction in table 7, there are clear gender differences in the emphasis members place on social welfare, feminist, and antifeminist initiatives. During both the 103rd and 104th Congresses, Democratic and Republican men across the ideological spectrum cosponsored more social welfare bills than feminist bills. Only liberal Democratic men in the 103rd Congress were evenly split in their attention to feminist and social welfare legislation.

By contrast, in the 103rd Congress, as a group, both Democratic and moderate Republican congresswomen on average cosponsored more feminist bills than social welfare bills. The openness of the Democratic

Table 7 The 103rd and 104th Congresses: Means for Feminist, Social Welfare, and Antifeminist Cosponsorship

	Democrat				Republican			
	Men		Women		Men		Women	
Bill Type	Conservative	Liberal	Conservative	Liberal	Conservative	Moderate	Conservative	Moderate
103rd Congress:								
Feminist	7	16	23	30.5	4	7.5	10	20
	(6)	(12)	(14)	(11.5)	(3)	(5)	(1)	(15)
Social welfare	9.5	16	13	21.5	10	11	11	15
	(7)	(10)	(6)	(10)	(4)	(6)	(4)	(7)
Antifeminist	.38	.03	0	0	3	1.3	1.5	1.1
	(.7)	(.18)			(1.4)	(.81)	(.58)	(1.1)
No. of representatives	72	150	5	30	119	44	4	8
104th Congress:								
Feminist	4.5	14.5	11	27	4	8	7	18
	(6)	(10)	(9)	(12)	(3)	(6)	(5)	(9)
Social welfare	12	19	14.5	22	14	16	15	20
	(7)	(10)	(6)	(10)	(7)	(8)	(4)	(6)
Antifeminist	1	.23	1	.04	6	2	6	1
	(1.5)	(.66)	(.82)	(.2)	(3)	(2)	(3)	(1.5)
No. of representatives	54	111	4	26	156	61	9	8

NOTE: Standard deviations are in parentheses.

party to feminist issues and the real potential that the Clinton administration would support these policies encouraged congresswomen to draft and/or sign on to proposals to expand family and medical leave, protect victims of domestic violence, support reproductive rights, and increase funding for women's health research. However, in the 104th Congress, as social conservatives gained control of the national policy agenda, only liberal Democratic women maintained their emphasis on feminist legislation. Both conservative Democratic women and Republican women cosponsored more social welfare proposals than feminist initiatives, with conservative Democratic women greatly reducing their support for feminist bills between the two Congresses. Yet, across both Congresses, moderate Republican women still cosponsored more feminist bills than did liberal Democratic men. Despite the widely varying political atmospheres of the two Congresses, moderate Republican women remained more open to feminist proposals than one would expect based on their party affiliation.

Finally, the results in table 7 indicate that in both the 103rd and 104th Congresses antifeminist legislation received the most support from conservative Republicans. These social conservatives used their majority power to pursue antifeminist goals particularly in the areas of abortion, homosexuality, and welfare reform. The new conservative women elected in the 104th Congress pursued antifeminist legislation just as actively as conservative Republican men did. The bills they cosponsored included the high-profile ban on partial birth abortions, the Republican Welfare Reform Bill, and the Defense of Marriage Act prohibiting gay marriage. They also cosponsored other bills prohibiting affirmative action, limiting the rights of homosexuals, banning sex education in the schools, prohibiting student participation in surveys without parental permission, and restricting abortion.[4] While the cosponsorship activity of liberal Democrats indicates that liberal Democratic women are more committed to the pursuit of feminist policies than are liberal Democratic men, the cosponsorship patterns of conservative Republicans demonstrate that conservative women and men are equally supportive of antifeminist positions. However, conservative women are not adopting a leadership role on these initiatives.

Unlike conservative Republican women, moderate Republican women generally limited their antifeminist cosponsorship to major party-backed initiatives that were cosponsored by a majority of the Republican Party Caucus. These bills included the Welfare Reform Bill, an antiaffirmative action bill, and the Family Reinforcement Act, a plank of the Contract with America, which included a provision requiring parental permission for student participation in all surveys. None of the senior moderate women signed on to the Defense of Marriage Act, and only declared pro-life advocate Ileana Ros-Lehtinen cosponsored the Partial Birth Abortion Act, even though many of these women sided with their party in the final roll-call vote. However, a small group of Democratic men defected from their party to cosponsor both the Partial Birth Abortion Act and the Defense of Marriage Act.[5]

Modeling Women's Issue Cosponsorship

To determine whether the gender differences found in tables 6 and 7 persist after accounting for the major factors that influence congressional decision making, I employ negative binomial regression models. The negative binomial is an event count model that allows one to model the number of bills that a member with a given set of characteristics will cosponsor in a given period of time.[6] The models in tables 8 and 9 evaluate the impact of gender on the decision to cosponsor the various types of women's issue bills after taking into account the major partisan, constituency, and institutional factors that guide the cosponsorship behavior of legislators.[7]

The statistics at the bottom of the tables give an overview of how well the models fit the data. The pseudo R^2 is a rough indicator of the amount of variation in the dependent variable explained by the model. The tables also include the correlation between the dependent variable, number of bills cosponsored, and the model predictions. Since the number of bills cosponsored by each member varies so widely, it is difficult for any model to predict accurately the exact number of bills that a member will cosponsor. For example, in the 103rd Congress, the number of women's issue bills cosponsored varies from one to 114 bills. The mode in table 8 indicates that at most, only eleven members cosponsored the same number of women's issue bills. In addition to the exact prediction, the tables report the number of members whose cosponsorship behavior the model predicts both within one bill and within five bills for the full set of women's issues and within two bills for the social welfare and feminist bills.[8]

As the interviews with members and current research on cosponsorship suggest, ideological views and party affiliation are the most important predictors of which bills a member will cosponsor. Across both Congresses, liberal Democrats cosponsor the most women's issue bills, both feminist and social welfare. Even after accounting for their liberal ideology, Democratic women are consistently more likely to cosponsor

Table 8   The 103rd and 104th Congresses: Negative Binomial Models on Women's Issue Bill Cosponsorship

Independent Variables	All Women's Issues			
	103rd Congress		104th Congress	
	Coefficient	Z-Statistic	Coefficient	Z-Statistic
Republican women	.606***	5.7	.586***	5.9
Democratic women	.384***	7.5	.254***	5.23
Republican men	.301***	3.69	.313***	3.7
Ideology	−.728***	−7.58	−.317***	−3.8
Freshman	.11**	3.14	.044	1.25
Southern	−.076+	−1.89	.048	1.38
Hispanic representative	.031	.39	.028	.38
% Vote Clinton	.272	1.1	.258	1.16
% Black	.098	.67	.104	.78
% Urban	.109	1.18	.067	.84
Median household income	−.013	−.54	.0003	.02
Woman's subcommittee	.116**	2.99	.133***	4.33
Woman's subcommittee chair	−.107	−.91	−.086	−.86
Woman's subcommittee ranking member	.106	.86	.014	.15
Woman's committee chair	.086	.73	.178+	1.66
Woman's committee ranking member	.034	.28	−.085	−.75
No. of bills cosponsored	.004***	27.71	.006***	31.34
Constant	1.49***	13.22	1.81***	16.49
Dispersion parameter	.046***	7.11	.029***	6.1
Pseudo-R^2	20		19	
Log likelihood	−1,432.97		−1,415.98	
Log likelihood ratio χ^2	702.08		664.19	
Correlation prediction & dependent variable	90.3		89.3	
Mode (members)	11		18	
Exact prediction (members)	30/432		29/429	
Prediction ± 1	92/432		69/429	
Prediction ± 5	270/432		251/429	

+$p \leq .01$.
*$p \leq .05$.
**$p \leq .01$.
***$p < .001$.

women's issue bills than are their male counterparts. Similarly, Republican congresswomen are consistently more active cosponsors of feminist and social welfare legislation than are Republican men.

To isolate the impact of being a woman on the number of women's issue bills a member will cosponsor, as in chapter 3, I calculated predicted probabilities for the number of women's issue, feminist, and social welfare bills that would be cosponsored by hypothetical male and female members who shared the same party and ideological views and who represented districts with the same level of Democratic support, as measured by the district's vote for Bill Clinton in 1992.[9] (Results not shown.) Across both Congresses, a liberal Democratic woman from a strongly Democratic district would always cosponsor more women's issue bills than a similarly situated Democratic man. Thus, in the 103rd Congress, on average, the liberal woman would cosponsor forty-one women's issue bills while the liberal man would cosponsor twenty-eight bills. During the 104th Congress, on average the liberal congresswoman would cosponsor thirty-four bills while the liberal congressman would cosponsor twenty-seven bills. Similarly, moderate Republican women who represent more Democratic districts than most Republicans would cosponsor more bills than similarly situated Republican men. The female moderate Republican representatives would cosponsor, on average, twenty-five bills in the 103rd Congress compared to eighteen bills by their male counterparts and would cosponsor thirty-one bills in the 104th Congress compared to twenty-four bills by the moderate Republican men.

Consistent with the bill sponsorship findings, interest in feminist initiatives constitutes the largest area of gender differences observed. For example, across both Congresses, liberal Democratic women cosponsored an average of seven to ten more feminist bills than did liberal Democratic men, and moderate Republican women cosponsored five to six more feminist bills than did moderate Republican men. While the analysis of bill sponsorship demonstrates that moderate Republican women drastically reduced their sponsorship of feminist legislation when they gained majority status, these same Republican women maintained their rate of cosponsorship, signing on to an average of eleven bills in the 103rd Congress and ten bills in the 104th Congress. It is possible that moderate Republican congresswomen, knowing that the majority did not favor feminist initiatives and loath to alienate important party constituencies, were less enthusiastic about drafting feminist proposals, but they continued to register their support for feminist initiatives through the less threatening medium of cosponsorship.

With regard to social welfare issues, the sex differences captured in the models translate into smaller differences of one to 3.5 bills cosponsored by men and women with similar ideologies who represent districts with equivalent levels of Democratic support. Yet liberal Democratic women and moderate Republican women are predicted to cosponsor

Table 9 The 103rd and 104th Congresses: Negative Binomial Models on Feminist and Social Welfare Cosponsorship

| | 103rd Congress | | | | 104th Congress | | | |
| | Feminist | | Social Welfare | | Feminist | | Social Welfare | |
Independent Variables	Coefficient	Z-Statistic	Coefficient	Z-Statistic	Coefficient	Z-Statistic	Coefficient	Z-Statistic
Republican women	1.05***	6.63	.38***	3.25	1.44***	8.57	.393***	3.43
Democratic women	.57***	8.02	.155**	2.84	.445***	6.14	.026	.45
Republican men	.205	1.62	.272**	3.08	.803***	5.44	.205*	2.11
Ideology	-1.42***	-9.43	-.575***	-5.53	-1.31***	-9.12	-.218*	-2.27
Freshman	.134*	2.53	.093*	2.45	.114+	1.82	.003	.06
Hispanic representative	-.007	-.06	.097	1.15	-.004	-.03	.052	.61
% Vote Clinton	-.108	-.29	.402	1.52	.623+	1.65	-.081	-.31
Southern	-.176**	2.82	-.016	-.38	.105+	1.67	.037	.92
% Urban	.152	1.08	-.0001	-.001	.152	1.09	.034	.37
% Black	.115	.53	.071	.45	-.293	-1.35	.266+	1.72
Median income	.041	1.11	-.041	-1.54	.079*	2.19	-.017	-.68
Feminist/social welfare subcommittee chair	.04	.67	.121**	2.85	.086	1.49	.168***	4.53
Feminist/social welfare subcommittee ranking member	-.36*	-1.99	-.11	-.77	-.06	-.29	.031	.26
Woman's committee chair	.247	1.3	.031	.17	-.27	-1.55	-.006	-.05
Woman's committee ranking member	.032	-.18	.191	1.45	-.126	-.482	.248*	2.14
	-.126	-.55	.212	1.63	-.282	-1.54	-.054	-.41

No. of bills cosponsored	.005***	20.58	.004***	24.47	.007***	21.2	.005***	25.48
Constant	.272	1.6	1.11***	9.17	−.143	−.77	1.67***	13.16
Dispersion parameter	.086***	6.1	.025***	3.69	.065***	5.05	.027***	4.28
Pseudo-R^2	22		19		22.5		16	
Log likelihood	−1,165.51		−1,191		−1,083.13		−1,252.85	
Log likelihood ratio χ^2	662.25		555.57		629.52		481.8	
Correlation prediction & dependent variable	88.3		86.6		88.3		82.5	
Mode (members)	36		32		46		26	
Exact prediction (members)	58/432		54/432		65/429		38/429	
Prediction ± 1	108		136		184		108	
Prediction ± 2	200		211		259		174	

[+] $p \leq .01$.
[*] $p \leq .05$.
[**] $p \leq .01$.
[***] $p < .001$.

more social welfare bills than any other category of members when their party holds power.[10] These women recognize that the agenda control wielded by the majority provides them with a more realistic chance of influencing the direction of policy in an area that has formed the center of party conflict since the New Deal. Therefore, these Democratic and Republican women are more motivated to spend time and political capital on these issues than are their male partisans only when they have access to the prerogatives of the majority.

In addition to ideology and gender, the models in table 8 and 9 highlight the ways in which members' position within the institution has an impact on their ability to pursue their legislative goals. Thus, freshmen are more likely to cosponsor all types of women's issue bills than are more senior members, while holding a committee leadership position is a generally insignificant and sometimes negative influence on women's issue cosponsorship. This finding reflects the fact that cosponsorship provides freshmen, who are still adjusting to the institution and are often relegated to less prestigious committees, with an opportunity to articulate their policy preferences. In contrast, the additional resources and agenda power that are controlled by committee leaders makes cosponsorship a less useful policy device for these members.

The significance of holding a seat on a women's issue subcommittee as a determinant of which members cosponsor women's issue bills reflects the influence of a legislator's committee position on the development of his or her priorities. The primary position that social welfare issues hold on the congressional agenda is reinforced by the fact that subcommittee membership is a pivotal influence on the decision to cosponsor a social welfare bill, but being a subcommittee member has no impact on which members cosponsor feminist initiatives. Since social welfare issues are well-integrated into committee agendas, this finding supports the assertion of researchers who claim that cosponsors are policy experts who are trying to send signals to their fellow representatives about the quality of a piece of legislation (Krehbiel 1995; Kessler and Krehbiel 1996).

Finally, as expected, legislators who cosponsor the full set of women's issue bills and social welfare bills tend to represent urban, low-income districts with high minority populations, while representatives who cosponsor feminist bills are more likely to hail from high-income districts. This situation may reflect the fact that social welfare programs are extremely important to low-income districts. Meanwhile, white liberal Democrats and moderate Republicans often represent districts that are wealthy and socially liberal.

Explaining Gender Differences in Cosponsorship

As research on cosponsorship indicates, there are two sides to the cosponsorship decision: the interests of the potential cosponsors and the desire of the bill's primary backers to send legislative signals to fellow representatives and the media about the quality and nature of support for a bill. Interviews with members and staff indicate that, in addition to a congresswoman's personal level of interest in pursuing women's issue policy goals or taking stands on these issues for constituents, some bill sponsors actively seek congresswomen's support on women's issue bills.

In some cases the bill sponsor wanted to enlist a congresswoman as a lead cosponsor because of her perceived expertise and connection to important interest groups. For example, a Republican subcommittee staffer explained that when the subcommittee chair decided the time was right to reform adoption laws, he chose to approach a specific Democratic congresswoman as a lead cosponsor because Democrats, particularly female Democrats, are "naturally interested in social issues like adoption." Also, the congresswoman had worked on an adoption bill in the early 1980s and if she agreed to the provisions, she could bring the Democratic interest groups, such as the Children's Defense Fund and the Child Welfare League, on board. Similarly, a Republican congressman said that he asked a particular Democratic congresswoman to be the lead Democratic cosponsor of his pediatric research initiative because she has a seat on the Rules Committee and she is recognized as a leader in children's health issues.

In other cases, bill proponents recruited women as cosponsors because they wanted to enlist them as symbols of moral authority on an issue. For example, a legislative assistant to a moderate Republican woman described the efforts she was making to get all congresswomen to sign on to a breast cancer bill. Her congresswoman had recently met with other Republican women to decide who should write Dear Colleague letters and who should talk to the four remaining Republican women who had not signed on to the bill. Similarly, particularly during the 103rd Congress, the Congressional Caucus for Women's Issues created omnibus legislative packages on issues including women's health, gender equity in education, and economic equity for women. The caucus leaders organized their members to sponsor and cosponsor each of these provisions to send a message to the media and fellow representatives that women cared about these issues and were united in support of this bill. This combination of interest, perceived expertise, and symbolic moral authority may contribute to the gender differences found in legislators' women's issue cosponsorship behavior.

Conclusion

While ideology is the most important factor driving legislators' cosponsorship decisions, the analysis of women's issue cosponsorship confirms that congresswomen are more likely to cosponsor women's issue bills than are their male partisan colleagues. These gender differences stem from the policy focus of the social liberals within each party as liberal Democratic women are even more likely to cosponsor women's issue bills than are liberal Democratic men, and moderate Republican women are more active proponents of women's issue legislation than are moderate Republican men.

Interview evidence and past research on cosponsorship suggests that cosponsorship serves both as a mechanism for individual members to register their opinions on an issue and as a way for bill sponsors to demonstrate the level of support behind their bills. Therefore, the gender differences found in representatives' cosponsorship behavior on women's issues may stem from a combination of congresswomen's personal policy interests and the efforts of bill sponsors, when building support for legislation, to capitalize on female representatives' perceived expertise and moral authority on these issues.

Chapter 5

Amendments in Committees:
Working behind the Scenes for Women's Issues

During the 103rd Congress, the appropriations bills funding the Departments of Labor, Health and Human Services, and Education included
a record $600 million for breast cancer research programs as well as
funding for breast and cervical cancer prevention programs and ovar-
ian cancer research. Participants in the appropriations process credited
the increased attention to women's health issues to the fact that the pre-
viously all-male subcommittee now included three Democratic women
and one Republican woman. These women, particularly the Democratic
women, worked to expand the portion of the budgetary pie devoted
to women's health (Margolies-Mezvinsky 1994; Dodson et al. 1995,
Dodson 1998).

Describing the overwhelming importance of a representative's committee assignment, one staffer asserted that a member "can be most
influential and can get the most done legislatively on [his or her] committee, otherwise you need to have a strong ally on another committee
if you want something done." Through their committee assignments,
legislators set the agenda and define the range of policy choices by
convening hearings, drafting bills, and moving or blocking legislation.
Committee members also have important informational advantages
over their colleagues due to their access to staff with issue expertise
and the competition among interest groups and agencies to provide
them with policy information. Committee and subcommittee chairs
wield even more control over policy outcomes through their ability
to convene a legislative markup on a bill and to recess that markup
if the process does not conform to their goals. Additionally, the chair
decides which proposals will be included in the "chairman's mark,"
the bill that is the focus of the committee markup (Fenno 1973; Smith
and Deering 1990; Hall 1996; Oleszek 1996). Scholars disagree over
the extent of committee autonomy in policy formation, describing

committees as agents of constituency service logrolls (Shepsle and Weingast 1987; Weingast and Marshall 1988), the policy preferences of the full House chamber (Krehbiel 1991, 1998), or the views of the majority party (Kiewiet and McCubbins 1991; Cox and McCubbins 1993; Aldrich and Rhode 2000), while others claim that their independence depends on the salience of the issue before the committee (Maltzman and Smith 1994; Maltzman 1995, 1997). However, all congressional observers recognize the value of a seat on the relevant committee to the achievement of a legislator's policy goals.

Since the committees are the center of policy development in Congress, I analyze amending behavior during committee markups, in this chapter, to determine whether congresswomen are more likely than their male colleagues are to use their committee positions to press for the inclusion of women's interests in committee legislation. I also examine how congresswomen's lack of access to important committees and committee leadership posts constrains their ability to translate their interest in women's issues into concrete legislative action. Finally, I demonstrate how partisan pressures and the priorities of the committee and subcommittee chair regulate a legislator's political calculus concerning the feasibility of achieving his or her policy goals.

Why Expect Congresswomen to Act as Advocates in Committee?

Among committee members, not all legislators participate in each policy debate. Even within a subcommittee, Hall (1996) found that only a small subset of interested members, whose preferences do not reflect the values of the chamber, actively participates in the development of legislation. The identity of this subset of members varies from bill to bill. Krehbiel (1991) refers to these activist members as information specializers whose interest in a policy area or personal background allows them to provide the entire chamber with reliable policy information. Shepsle and Weingast (1987) characterize these members as preference outliers whose districts have a particular stake in a policy area. It is possible that personal experience or a desire to represent women as a national constituency will lead female representatives to take a more active interest in policy development on women's issues than will their fellow committee members. One Democratic congresswoman explained, "as the only woman on the—Committee for many years, I was the only one thinking from a woman's point of view so I had to be responsible for bringing women and family issues to the table on top of everything else," such as district and other policy interests. Therefore, throughout her tenure, she tried to use the tax code to help families, championing issues like the Earned Income Tax Credit and a child-care tax credit.

Any personal commitment that congresswomen display toward women's issues will be augmented by the lobbying efforts of women's groups and other social welfare–oriented groups. In their study of interest group behavior, Hall and Wayman (1990) assert that the main goal of interest groups is not to buy votes but to buy time to convince members to become champions of their issues and to guide their favored policies through the committee process. Social welfare interest groups and women's groups, particularly feminist organizations who have PACs dedicated to electing women, may view female members as the most sympathetic to their cause and will actively seek their support for women's issue initiatives. Consequently, female committee members, particularly majority party members, will be offered more opportunities to become champions of women's issue legislation than will the average member. Indeed, in interviews, several moderate Republican women maintained that when the Republicans gained the majority, they were bombarded with requests from women's issue interest groups seeking their help to save their programs from conservative Republican cuts.

The Existing Evidence concerning the Influence of Female Legislators in Committees

Given the institutional advantages held by committee members, it is clear that the composition of the committees, particularly the identity of subcommittee members and committee leaders, is a key determinant of policy outcomes. However, there are relatively few studies that focus on the behavior of women in committees. Some scholars maintain that women bring a unique style of leadership to their legislative work. For example, in her analysis of committee hearings in the Colorado state legislature, Kathlene (1994, 1998) found that female chairs were less likely than male chairs to interrupt their colleagues and they exhibited a more collegial leadership style. Similarly, Rosenthal (1997, 1998) also asserts that female committee chairs exhibit a more inclusive working style that incorporates colleagues and peers in committee activities and focuses on public involvement in the committee process. However, this relationship only held in the less professionalized state legislatures.

With regard to policy development, in her analysis of crime policy in the Colorado legislature, Kathlene (1995, 1998) maintains that female committee members were guided by an "ethic of care" that led them to focus more on prevention and rehabilitation proposals while men relied on an "ethic of justice" and "abstract rights," which led them to offer more proposals to expand punishment. In her study of state legislatures, Thomas (1994) observed that female state legislators were more likely than men to hold a seat on a health and welfare committee and to chair this type of committee, thus reinforcing the idea that women demonstrate more interest in policies related to their traditional role as caregivers. Moreover, in their study of abortion policies across the states, Berkman and O'Connor (1993) found that Democratic women used their committee seats to block pro-life legislation in state legislatures, particularly in states with fewer female legislators and in states that are more likely to support policies restricting abortion.

At the congressional level, case studies indicate that, in the 103rd Congress, Democratic women with seats on the relevant committees played essential roles in incorporating women's health concerns into the committee markups of the Clinton health reform bill and in shepherding the Freedom of Access to Abortion Clinic Entrances Act and the Violence against Women Act through committee and floor passage (Dodson et al. 1995; Dodson 1998, 2000). In the 104th Congress, the Republican women who held key positions in the leadership and on the Ways and Means Committee were able to moderate the welfare reform bill, and they successfully included provisions for victims of domestic violence in the health insurance portability legislation (Dodson 1997; Casey and Carroll 1998; Norton 2002). Finally, in her study of reproductive policy legislation from 1969 to 1992, Norton (1994, 1995, 1999, 2002) found that in almost all cases, subcommittee members pushed their preferences on reproductive policy through the floor debate and conference committee regardless of the will of the majority in Congress or the president's policy priorities. Generally congresswomen did not hold seats on these influential subcommittees and thus were excluded from meaningful participation in reproductive policy debates.

The small number of studies on the behavior of women in committee demonstrates the need for a systematic analysis of the impact of social identity on members' committee priorities. In this chapter, I examine the amending activity of representatives during committee markups to evaluate whether congresswomen are using their committee seats to advocate for the inclusion of women's issues in committee legislation. Information from the interviews provides insights into the obstacles legislators face from their parties and from committee and subcommittee leaders as they work to incorporate their women's issue proposals into committee legislation.

Identifying Women's Issue Amendments

Among the hundreds of bills that members sponsor in each session of Congress, very few receive consideration by the committees. Only about 11 percent of the more than five hundred women's issue initiatives offered in each Congress advanced to a committee markup, fifty-eight bills in the 103rd Congress and sixty-three bills in the 104th Congress.[1] I examined the amendments proposed during each markup session to identify those that concerned women's issues and to categorize amendments as social welfare, feminist, and antifeminist.[2] On many occasions, committees approve legislation without amendment. Thus, the number of amendments offered to a bill ranged from zero to 219 amendments in eight committees for the Clinton Health Care Reform Bill during the 103rd Congress, and ninety-six amendments in five committees for the final Republican Welfare Reform Bill during the 104th Congress.

Furthermore, many amendments proposed to a bill do not concern women's issues. For example, the sample for the 103rd Congress includes amendments to the Democrats' Crime Bill, which concerned crimes against women, children, and the elderly. However, I excluded the numerous amendments concerning such issues as prison construction and minimum mandatory sentences for violent crimes. The final sample of women's issue amendments includes 447 amendments offered by 126 members of the 103rd Congress and 588 amendments offered by 171 members of the 104th Congress.[3] Appendix B provides a detailed listing of the bills and the number of amendments offered in each markup.

Understanding the Advantages and Limitations of Committee Markup Data

Analyzing the amendments offered by members during the committee markup provides a good measure of interest in women's issues. Unlike floor activity, which can be limited by restrictive rules dictating the number of amendments that can be offered to a bill, generally any committee member that attends the markup can offer an amendment to the bill. However, the markup process does not allow representatives the complete freedom to express their policy preferences that bill sponsorship and cosponsorship provide, since legislators can only offer amendments to a bill if they are members of the committee with jurisdiction.

In addition, the opportunities to amend legislation depend on the decisions made by party leaders and committee and subcommittee chairs concerning whether to bring legislation up for a markup. The actions of congressional leaders are guided by their assessment of the priorities of the president, the electoral needs of the party, and the standing policy responsibilities of the committee (Fenno 1973; Smith and Deering 1990; Hall 1996; Oleszek 1996). For example, in the 103rd Congress, President Clinton's desire to create a national health insurance plan led Democratic leaders to put the Clinton Health Reform Bill on the fast track (Skocpol 1997). Therefore, the Education and Labor Committee was one of eight committees that considered the far-reaching bill. Members of this committee also had to fulfill their responsibility to reauthorize the programs in the 1965 Elementary and Secondary Education Act, and they had to achieve the president's goal of creating a new national service program, Americorps (Waldman 1995). Similarly, during the 104th Congress, Republican leaders, flush with the excitement of ascending to the majority after forty years in the minority, were anxious to solidify their popularity with the voters by delivering on the items in the Contract with America, including welfare reform. Therefore, the Ways and Means Committee was given leading responsibility in the consideration of several iterations of the Republican Welfare Reform Bill, a process that ultimately involved five different committees. Members of Ways and Means also held responsibility for the Medicare overhaul, a cornerstone of Republican efforts to balance the federal budget and achieve reform of the health care system where Democrats had failed (Gimpel 1996; Maraniss and Weisskopf 1996; Killian 1998).

One potential drawback to analyzing committee amending activity, however, is that one does not capture any premarkup activity in which members work to convince the chair to include their proposals in the chairman's mark, the bill that will be subject to amendment during the markup. Members of the majority party are most likely to convince the chair to include their proposals in a bill, obviating the need for amendments. Thus, measuring amending behavior in committees may slightly discount the influence of majority party membership.

Another problem with reliance on committee data is that observers of the 104th Congress frequently point to a loss of committee power during this session and an increased centralization of control in the party leadership. To insure loyalty to the leadership, Speaker Gingrich ignored the seniority system and appointed conservative loyalists as chairs of the Commerce, Judiciary, and Appropriations Committees. The committee staffs that help committee leaders and rank-and-file members gather information and draft alternative proposals were cut by one-third. Gingrich also created more than twenty-five party task forces that were directly accountable to the Speaker to formulate policy on issues ranging from Medicare and welfare reform to the dismantling of the Department of Education (Aldrich and Rhode 1997, 2000; Evans and Oleszek 1997). The purpose of these task forces was "to press committees to consider issues and arrive at decisions close to the leadership's positions, with the implied threat that if committees did not deliver the appropriate legislation, they would be bypassed" (Owens 1997, 261). Particularly with respect to items in the Contract with America, committee chairs were compelled to expedite the process by holding abbreviated hearings and sometimes skipping subcommittee markups.

This shift in power to the party leadership, however, does not affect the current analysis of committee markup data because it measures interest in women's issues and not final influence over policy outcomes. Most bills that were reported on the floor were marked up in committee, and even 90 percent of the bills in the Contract with America were subject to extensive amending proposals in committee markup (Owens 1997). Therefore, the committee markup was the one place that all members, particularly Democrats, could express their views on a bill and register dissent.

Thus, the analysis of committee amending behavior will reveal whether female committee members are more committed to pursuing women's interests than are their male counterparts. Additionally, an investigation of committee behavior can also indicate whether congresswomen are bringing their gender-related concerns to debates in committees that do not consider a large amount of gender-related legislation.

Comparing Gender Differences in Women's Issue Amending Behavior

Tables 10 and 11 provide a general overview of the committee amending data cross-tabulated by gender and party. There are several significant patterns in the charts. First, the data in table 10 demonstrates that all members increased their amending activity in the 104th Congress, with the largest increase among Democrats.[4] In both Congresses, Democratic women were the most active sponsors as a proportion of their group, with 36 percent in the 103rd and 55 percent in the 104th offering women's issue amendments.

The dramatic increase in Democratic amending behavior captures Democrats' reaction to their new minority status and the activist Republican policy agenda. After forty years in the minority, Republicans pursued their goal of dismantling the welfare state by concentrating

Table 10 The 103rd and 104th Congresses: Women's Issue Amendment Sponsorship

	Democratic				Republican			
	Men (103rd $N = 222$; 104th $N = 165$)		Women (103rd $N = 36$; 104th $N = 31$)		Men (103rd $N = 163$; 104th $N = 217$)		Women (103rd $N = 12$; 104th $N = 17$)	
	Sponsor (%)	Ams.	Sponsor (%)	Ams.	Sponsor (%)	Ams.	Sponsor (%)	Ams.
103rd Congress	28	199	36	41	30	189	25	18
104th Congress	45	332	55	76	34	162	35	18

NOTE: N = Number of members in the category. Thus, there were 222 Democratic men serving in the 103rd Congress. Ams. = Amendments.

their attention on reforming social programs including AFDC, Medicare, and Medicaid. Democrats were equally determined to protect these cherished programs. The ideological polarization in the House and Speaker Gingrich's efforts to centralize party control through the use of party task forces and close consultation between committee chairs and the leadership concerning bill content meant that the committee markup was the one place where Democrats could express their opposition and attempt to influence policy.

To advance their conservative policy goals concerning women's issues further, Republican leaders aggressively employed legislative riders on appropriations bills. By attaching controversial social provisions to the appropriations bills instead of passing them as separate pieces of legislation, the Republican leadership hoped to force President Clinton to accept their policy goals rather than risk a government shutdown. This strategy heightened tensions on the traditionally bipartisan Appropriations Committee and led to very contentious markup sessions (Maraniss and Weisskopf 1996; Aldrich and Rhode 2000). For example, under Democratic leadership in the 103rd Congress, the two Labor, Health and Human Services, and Education (LHHS) appropriations bills attracted only eight women's issue amendments. By contrast, forty-three women's issue amendments were offered to these same two bills in the 104th Congress.

Republicans were especially active in the area of abortion. For example, they used the LHHS appropriations bills to try to eliminate Title X family planning programs and transfer the funds to maternal and child health grants, to eliminate the rape and incest exceptions for Medicaid coverage of abortion, to prohibit fetal tissue research, and to exempt

Table 11 The 103rd and 104th Congresses: Feminist, Social Welfare, and Antifeminist Amendment Sponsorship

	Democratic				Republican			
	Men (103rd $N=222$; 104th $N=165$)		Women (103rd $N=36$; 104th $N=31$)		Men (103rd $N=163$; 104th $N=217$)		Women (103rd $N=12$; 104th $N=17$)	
Issue Type	Sponsor (%)	Ams.	Sponsor (%)	Ams.	Sponsor (%)	Ams.	Sponsor (%)	Ams.
103rd Congress:								
Feminist committee & floor	12	44	31	21	6	12	33	5
Social welfare	21	150	17	21	23	144	25	13
Antifeminist committee & floor	2	6	0	0	13.5	44	17	2
104th Congress:								
Feminist committee & floor	19	51	39	46	11	31	35	10
Social welfare	42	278	52	45	29	115	29	13
Antifeminist committee & floor	1	2	0	0	9	32	0	0

NOTE: N = Number of members in the category. Thus, there were 222 Democratic men serving in the 103rd Congress. Ams. = Amendments.

schools and teaching hospitals from losing their federal funding if they refused to perform abortions. The three Democratic women on the Labor, Health and Human Services, and Education Subcommittee, Congresswomen Nita Lowey (D-NY), Rosa DeLauro (D-CT), and Nancy Pelosi (D-CA), were particularly active in their efforts to block these initiatives (Clemmit, Primmer, and Simms 1997).

Investigating Gender Differences in Committee Amending Behavior by Policy Area

In table 11, I divide the women's issue amendments by policy area to examine gender differences in the priority representatives place on feminist, social welfare, and antifeminist proposals. To increase the sample of feminist and antifeminist amendments, I combined the number of these proposals that legislators offered both in committee and on the floor. As with the bill sponsorship and cosponsorship data, table 11 demonstrates that across the two Congresses, both Democratic and Republican men offered more social welfare amendments than feminist amendments, while a larger proportion of Democratic and Republican women focused their attention on bringing feminist issues to the committee agenda. The approximately 20 percent gap between the percentage of Republican men sponsoring social welfare and those sponsoring feminist committee amendments in the 103rd and 104th Congresses is the largest among the four groups. This result is not surprising since feminist amendments generally reflect liberal policy goals that are associated with the Democratic Party. The feminist initiatives included such proposals as efforts to include coverage of abortion services in the Clinton Health Reform Bill, to expand research on women's health, to expand family and medical leave, to protect women who are victims of sexual harassment in the military, to expand affirmative action programs for women-owned businesses and women scientists, to create additional gender equity programs in education, to increase child-support enforcement, to protect job training programs for divorced homemakers, and to increase funding for child-care services to women on welfare.

While all members proposed more social welfare amendments than feminist amendments in the 104th Congress, the small group of Democratic women sponsored almost as many feminist amendments as their more numerous male Democratic colleagues did. In both Congresses, the proportion of Republican women offering feminist and social welfare amendments is almost equal. Thus, Republican women appear to maintain the same level of commitment to feminist issues even when their party gained the majority and the costs of antagonizing important majority coalition supporters increased. Furthermore, Republican women are less active sponsors of antifeminist amendments than Republican men are across both Congresses. While Republican men actively pursued initiatives to restrict abortion rights, scale back gender equity programs in education and athletics, prohibit benefits to homosexual partners, and deny welfare benefits to teens, only two Republican women in the 103rd Congress offered antifeminist amendments in committee.[5] None of the new conservative women elected in the 104th Congress sponsored an antifeminist amendment in committee or on the floor, while four of their male counterparts initiated antifeminist proposals. However, this fact may reflect a lack of opportunity rather than a lack of commitment to antifeminist causes, since none of the new conservative women held a seat on one of the subcommittees that considered the most women's issue legislation.[6]

Modeling Committee Amending Behavior on Women's Issues

Once the major factors that guide the legislative choices of representatives are accounted for, it is possible that the gender differences found in tables 10 and 11 actually reflect legislator's committee responsibilities and the needs of their district rather than the unique influence of social identity. Therefore, I utilize ordered logit models to discern the characteristics of members who initiate women's issue amendments.[7] The PRE (Proportionate Reduction in Error) statistic indicates how much better the model predicts women's issue amendment sponsorship than if one were to just guess the mode.[8] Since legislators generally do not sponsor women's issue amendments, the mode is always zero, and the models demonstrate which factors encourage a legislator to propose a women's issue amendment in committee.

   The models in tables 12 and 13 highlight the important legislative advantages commanded by members who hold seats on key subcommittees or occupy committee leadership posts. The legislators who sat on the subcommittees that considered the most women's issue legislation were always the most active sponsors of all types of women's issue amendments during the full committee markup. Beyond the rank-and-file committee members, the committee and subcommittee leaders utilized their considerable procedural advantages to shape policy outcomes. The committee chairs lead the markup sessions and often propose manager's amendments that incorporate last minute deals into the bill while ranking members lead the minority party's effort

Table 12 The 103rd and 104th Congresses Ordered Logits on Women's Issue Committee Amendments

Independent Variables	All Committee Amendments	
	103rd Congress	104th Congress
Republican women	.154	1.44[+]
	(.164)	(1.65)
Democratic women	.554	.9[+]
	(1.17)	(1.93)
Republican men	1.05[+]	1.2[+]
	(1.62)	(−1.67)
Ideology	−.477	−1.73*
	(−.62)	(−2.39)
Freshman	−.259	−.531
	(−.79)	(−1.62)
Southern	−.137	.567[+]
	(−.42)	(1.93)
% Vote for Clinton	−.097	3
	(−.05)	(1.56)
% Urban	.741	.476
	(1.01)	(.72)
% Black	.48	−3.59***
	(.4)	(−3.19)
Median household income	−.426*	.045
	(−2.08)	(.26)
Woman's subcommittee	2***	2.55***
	(9.04)	(9.61)
Woman's subcommittee ranking member	All sponsor	.358
		(.41)
Woman's committee chair	2.23**	All sponsor
	(2.6)	
Woman's committee ranking member	3.53**	1.95[+]
	(2.91)	(1.86)
No. of bills	.046***	.033**
	(3.69)	(2.49)
Number of observations	432	429
% Correct	75	71
PRE statistic (%)	13	28
PRE ± 1 (%)	32	49

NOTE: Numbers in parentheses are *Z*-statistics (coefficient/standard errors). "All sponsor" indicates that all members in the category sponsored an amendment; therefore, since there is no variation in the data, a coefficient cannot be estimated.

[+] $p \leq .1$.

* $p \leq .05$.

** $p \leq .01$.

*** $p \leq .001$.

Table 13   The 103rd and 104th Congresses Feminist and Social Welfare Amendments

Independent Variables	103rd Committee & Floor Feminist	103rd Committee Social Welfare	104th Committee & Floor Feminist	104th Committee Social Welfare
Republican women	2.26*	.096	3.43**	1.44
	(2.16)	(.09)	(2.9)	(1.6)
Democratic women	1.37**	−.157	1.28**	.464
	(2.75)	(−.26)	(2.61)	(1.03)
Republican men	.73	1.01	1.81+	1.4+
	(.72)	(1.36)	(−1.63)	(1.89)
Ideology	−1.34	−.41	−2.75**	−2.13**
	(−1.16)	(−.45)	(−2.58)	(−2.88)
Freshman	−.004	−.214	−.149	−.244
	(−.01)	(−.55)	(−.33)	(−.72)
% Hispanic	2.45+	.93	.958	.731
	(1.88)	(.78)	(.76)	(.79)
Southern	−.596	−.255	−.203	.383
	(−1.13)	(−.66)	(−.46)	(1.22)
% Vote for Clinton	−.478	−1.04	−3.45	2.81
	(−.17)	(−.43)	(−1.29)	(1.44)
% Urban	.487	−.14	.582	.213
	(.38)	(−.01)	(.55)	(.28)
% Black	.437	.994	.508	−3.45**
	(.25)	(.64)	(.32)	(−2.78)
Median household income	−.005	−.745**	.434+	−.127
	(−.02)	(−2.67)	(1.78)	(−.64)
Feminist/woman's subcommittee	.65	2.29***	2.35***	2.22***
	(1.61)	(9.29)	(7.16)	(8.33)
Feminist/woman's subcommittee chair	2.71**	−.655	−.15	.111
	(3.17)	(−.94)	(−.15)	(.16)
Feminist/woman's subcommittee ranking member	1.87+	.963	1.39	.821
	(1.9)	(.94)	(1.59)	(.94)
Woman's committee chair	1.71*	2.58**	.919	3.24*
	(2.38)	(2.86)	(1.07)	(2.38)
Woman's committee ranking member	2.27**	4.56***	.395	2.07+
	(2.67)	(3.62)	(.46)	(1.9)
No. of bills	.047**	.043**	.012	.033*
	(3.06)	(3.08)	(.64)	(2.48)
Number of observations	432	432	429	429
% Correct	90	81	87	71
PRE statistic (%)	14	14	19	21
PRE ± 1 (%)	22	31	31	43

NOTE: Numbers in parentheses are Z-statistics (coefficient/standard errors).
+ $p \leq .1$.
* $p \leq .05$.
** $p \leq .01$.
*** $p \leq .001$.

to eliminate offensive provisions and attach initiatives that will alter the content of the bill to better reflect the minority position. The overwhelming importance of subcommittee position and committee leadership roles indicates that where one sits within the institution imposes an important constraint on that legislator's ability to pursue his or her policy goals on women's issues regardless of his or her abstract preferences. Therefore, the composition of the committee membership and the selection of panel leaders are key determinants of policy outcomes.

In addition to subcommittee members and committee leaders, minority party legislators—Republicans in the 103rd Congress and Democrats in the 104th Congress—are among the most active participants in committee markups on women's issue bills. With regard to the 103rd Congress, Republican men were the most unhappy with Democratic initiatives on women's issues; therefore, these minority party legislators were the most likely to advance women's issue amendments in committee. In the more ideological 104th Congress, the combination of party and the DW-NOMINATE ideology scores demonstrates that liberal Democrats were the most likely to lead the charge against Republican policies by sponsoring women's issue amendments, both feminist and social welfare. Once the ideological component of party affiliation is accounted for, the party coefficients demonstrate that moderate Republican men and women were more likely to offer women's issue amendments than were conservative Democratic men.

The activism of minority party members shows that the committee markups provided a forum for these legislators to express their opposition to the majority party agenda. Thus, in the 103rd Congress, Republicans actively sought to limit Clinton's national health insurance program, to reduce the impact of the Family and Medical Leave Act on small businesses, and to reverse the expansion of federal education programs. Similarly, in the 104th Congress, Democrats offered amendments to modify the Republican Welfare Reform Bill, to reverse cuts in Medicare funding, and to weaken the Partial Birth Abortion Act by including provisions to protect the health of the mother.

Even after accounting for the advantages of subcommittee membership and the greater activism of minority party members, the regression results demonstrate that congresswomen do use their committee positions to advocate for women's interests. Additionally, congresswomen bring gender-related concerns to the policy debates of committees and subcommittees that do not have broad jurisdiction over women's issues. As shown in table 12, Democratic women sponsored even more women's issue amendments than did their male counterparts with the same jurisdictional responsibilities. When Democratic women were relegated to the minority party in the 104th Congress, they were even more forceful in their opposition to Republican proposals on women's issues than were their male Democratic colleagues. In the 103rd Congress, the positive although insignificant coefficient for Democratic women suggests that as members of the majority, these congresswomen tried to convince their fellow Democrats to move more aggressively to advance what they perceived as women's interests.[9]

In contrast to the behavior of Democratic women, Republican congresswomen were not more aggressive advocates of women's issue amendments when they were in the minority. In fact, the regression results suggest that as minority party members, Republican women were less active sponsors of women's issue amendments than were Republican men, indicating that they were not as dissatisfied with Democratic initiatives on women's issues as their male colleagues were. When their party gained the majority in the 104th Congress, both moderate Republican women and men used the amending process to try to moderate their party's conservative proposals on women's issues. In both Congresses, however, the coefficients for Republican women are not strongly significant.

The instability of the coefficients for Republican women may be due to the fact that there are such a small number of Republican women in Congress: twelve in the 103rd Congress and seventeen in the 104th Congress, and an even smaller number of these women served on the women's issue subcommittees. A closer examination of the amending activity of Republican women indicates that the few Republican women who held seats on women's issue subcommittees actively pursued gender-related amendments. Thus, three of the four Republican women with seats on a relevant subcommittee in the 103rd Congress and all four of the Republican women with seats on a relevant subcommittee in the 104th Congress sponsored two or more women's issue amendments. In contrast to the activism of the Republican women with seats on the relevant subcommittees, the other Republican women largely remained silent on women's issues. Only two of the thirteen women who did not serve on a women's issue subcommittee in the 104th Congress offered a gender-related amendment. The commitment to gender-related initiatives displayed by those Republican women who served on women's issue subcommittees demonstrates that the inclusion of more women on influential committees and subcommittees could make the congressional agenda more responsive to women's interests.

When the women's issue amendments are divided by policy area into feminist and social welfare initiatives in table 13, the results demonstrate that the importance of social identity derives from congresswomen's commitment to the pursuit of feminist initiatives. While committee position, minority party status, and constituency interests are the most important determinants of which members will pursue social welfare initiatives, having a woman on the committee is a key indicator of whether a member will offer a feminist amendment. Thus, in the 103rd Congress, Democratic women tried to encourage their male colleagues to incorporate feminist concerns into Democratic legislative initiatives and they aggressively fought against conservative Republican proposals in the 104th Congress. Moderate Republican women maintained a commitment to pursuing feminist amendments even when they gained the majority, and such amendments ran against the will of the Republican caucus and important party constituencies, particularly social conservative interest groups. These women were even more aggressive proponents of feminist initiatives than were moderate Republican men.

As majority party members, Republican women had to fight against their own party members to incorporate feminist amendments into legislation. This conflict is particularly evident in the case of welfare reform, a centerpiece of the Republican Contract with America. Three of the four Republican women who offered feminist amendments offered amendments concerning child-support enforcement and child-care funding to the Republican welfare reform bill. Case studies of the development of welfare reform indicate that Republican women with seats on key committees, particularly Nancy Johnson (CT) and Jennifer Dunn (WA) of Ways and Means, worked to moderate the Republican welfare reform bill by convincing their male colleagues to increase funding for child care, strengthen child-support enforcement, and preserve Medicaid coverage for older children and women (Casey and Carroll 1998; Norton 2002).

Finally, the gender differences found in the committee amending behavior of representatives support the notion that congresswomen will bring women's interests to their committee deliberations regardless of the committee's jurisdiction (Kathlene 1994, 1998; Dodson et al. 1995; Dodson 1998, 2000; Norton 2002). For example, in committee debate over product liability reform, several Democratic women offered amendments to eliminate a Republican provision that capped noneconomic damages and tied punitive damages to economic losses. These women argued that such a cap would hurt individuals with low incomes, a group disproportionately composed of women, children, and the elderly (Women's Policy, Inc. 1996). Similarly, a Democratic woman who served on the Intelligence Committee championed the cause of pensions for widows and divorced spouses, while a Republican woman on the Science Committee used her position to find ways for the government to encourage more women to enter scientific careers.[10]

While committee and subcommittee leaders clearly command important advantages in the markup process, in the 103rd and 104th Congresses, none of the congresswomen chaired a major committee or subcommittee that had jurisdiction over women's issue legislation. The overwhelming importance of these subcommittee and committee leadership roles indicates that where one sits within the institution exercises an important constraint on whether a member can pursue preferences based on women's issues regardless of their desire to work on these matters.

What If There Were More Women on the Committee?

In the wake of the Clarence Thomas–Anita Hill hearings, the National Women's Political Caucus published a full-page advertisement in the *New York Times* asking, "What if fourteen women, instead of fourteen men, had sat on the Senate Judiciary Committee during the Clarence Thomas confirmation hearings?" (Burrell 1994). To evaluate the impact of having more women on those committees and subcommittees with jurisdiction over the most women's issue legislation, I developed predicted probabilities that measure how likely it is that a hypothetical male or female representative will sponsor a women's issue amendment.

Figure 6 displays these probabilities for the women's issue model for the 104th Congress, in which being a Democratic woman is a significant predictor of amending behavior. The graph indicates the likelihood that a congressman or congresswoman with a given party affiliation, ideological stance, level of Democratic support in the district, and subcommittee position will offer a women's issue amendment. Since the level of Democratic support in the district was not an important predictor of which members will sponsor a feminist amendment, the graphs in figures 7 and 8 indicate the likelihood that a male or female member with a given party affiliation, ideology, and subcommittee seat will offer a feminist amendment in committee or on the floor.[11]

The results displayed in figure 6 demonstrate that members who serve on subcommittees that consider the most women's issue legislation

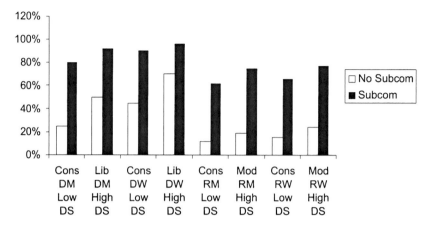

Figure 6   The 104th Congress: Probability of Sponsoring a Women's Issue Committee Amendment

NOTE: *Cons* = conservative; *Lib* = liberal; *Mod* = moderate; *DM* = Democratic men; *DW* = Democratic women; *RM* = Republican men; *RW* = Republican women; *Low DS* = low-level of Democratic support in the district; and *High DS* = high-level of Democratic support in the district. The bars represent the mean probability that a member with a given gender, party, ideology, subcommittee seat, and level of Democratic support in the district, as measured by the district vote for Bill Clinton in 1992, will offer a women's issue amendment in committee. To characterize members as hypothetical liberal or conservative Democrats and moderate or conservative Republicans, the ideology scores are set at the 25 percent and 75 percent quartiles within each party. Similarly, members are assigned a high or low level of district support for Democrats by setting the vote for Clinton at the 25 percent and 75 percent quartile levels within each party.

are the most likely to offer women's issue amendments during the full committee markup. Within the subcommittees, the minority party members, Democrats, are the most likely to initiate amendments because they are the most dissatisfied with Republican policy proposals. Therefore, minority Democrats who did not have access to majority party policy meetings or the chairman's mark would use their amendments to try to alter the committee bill or to force Republicans to take difficult votes that Democrats could use against them in the next election. On the Republican side, moderate Republicans from districts with higher levels of Democratic support than most districts represented by Republicans were the most active participants in the markup process.[12]

Among nonsubcommittee members, only liberal Democrats from strongly Democratic districts exhibit a 50 percent chance of sponsoring a women's issue amendment in committee. The liberal Democratic

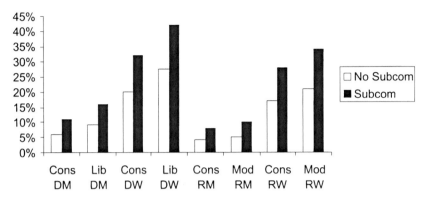

Figure 7   The 103rd Congress: Probability of Sponsoring a Feminist Committee or Floor
Amendment

NOTE: *Cons* = conservative; *Lib* = liberal; *Mod* = moderate; *DM* = Democratic men; *DW* =
Democratic women; *RM* = Republican men; and *RW* = Republican women. The bars represent the mean probability that a member with a given gender, party, ideology, and subcommittee seat will offer a feminist amendment in committee or on the floor. To characterize
members as hypothetical liberal or conservative Democrats and moderate or conservative
Republicans, the ideology scores are set at the 25 percent and 75 percent quartiles within each
party.

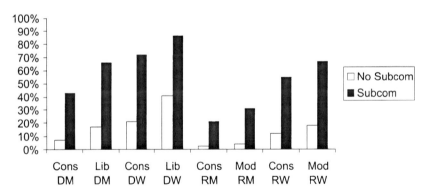

Figure 8   The 104th Congress: Probability of Sponsoring a Feminist Committee or Floor
Amendment

NOTE: *Cons* = conservative; *Lib* = liberal; *Mod* = moderate; *DM* = Democratic men; *DW* =
Democratic women; *RM* = Republican men; *RW* = Republican women. The bars represent the
mean probability that a member with a given gender, party, ideology, and subcommittee seat
will offer a feminist amendment in committee or on the floor. To characterize members as hypothetical liberal or conservative Democrats and moderate or conservative Republicans, the
ideology scores are set at the 25 percent and 75 percent quartiles within each party.

women are 20 percent more likely to offer an amendment than are liberal Democratic men. These Democratic women used their committee positions to combat Republican initiatives on health care, welfare, and abortion. For example, they offered numerous amendments to try to soften the Welfare Reform Bill by restoring benefits, expanding child care, and strengthening child-support enforcement.

As shown in figures 7 and 8, the most dramatic impact of the presence of women on committees is reflected in the sponsorship of feminist amendments. Across both Congresses, Democratic and Republican women were more likely to pursue feminist amendments than men were. In the 103rd Congress, only Democratic women who served on relevant subcommittees approached a 50 percent chance of sponsoring a feminist amendment in committee and on the floor. The activism of Democratic women indicates that even when their party held the majority, Democratic women were trying to move their party's committee legislation in a more feminist direction. For example, Democratic women offered amendments to establish programs for gender equity in education and to expand coverage of women's health services in the Clinton Health Reform Bill.

In the 104th Congress, the prominent position of social conservatives within the Republican Party Caucus led Republicans to draft policies that incorporated numerous antifeminist initiatives. The aggressive pursuit of socially conservative goals raised the stakes of conflict and more members became involved in committee debates on feminist issues. Indeed, liberal Democratic men serving on relevant subcommittees exhibited a 66 percent chance of sponsoring a feminist amendment in committee or on the floor. Congresswomen were even more committed to the pursuit of feminist causes than were their male colleagues. Female liberal Democratic subcommittee members were 20 percent more likely to offer a feminist amendment than were their liberal male colleagues, and conservative Democratic women were also more aggressive proponents of feminist amendments than were liberal Democratic men. Similarly, moderate Republican women serving on a relevant subcommittee were 36 percent more likely to sponsor feminist amendments than were moderate Republican men, and they were just as likely to offer a feminist amendment as liberal Democratic men. These Republican women focused their efforts on moderating the Republican Welfare Reform Bill and protecting reproductive rights. Thus, the predicted probabilities indicate that increasing the presence of women on relevant subcommittees could lead to more attention to women's issues, particularly feminist issues.

Partisan and Institutional Constraints Faced by Committee Members

The regression models and the predicted probabilities provide support for the notion that increasing women's presence on key committees and subcommittees will improve congressional attention to women's issues. Yet, in their efforts to pursue their policy goals, individual committee members are highly constrained by the policy preferences of the committee chairs and partisan colleagues on and off the committee. Since committee and subcommittee chairs act as the gatekeepers of which legislation will be called up for a markup and which proposals will be included in the chairman's mark, committee members are always mindful of maintaining a good relationship with the chair. As one staffer explained: "The support of the chair is especially sought after because if the chair will put it [the proposal] in his mark then it is in the bill and it is hard to remove. Otherwise you have to offer it as an amendment and that is harder to build support for. The chair can make this as easy or hard for you as he wants. He can make you jump through hoops and add fire to the hoops by challenging the germaneness of the amendment and things like that." The risks of antagonizing the chair are compounded by the fact that those members who oppose the chair often find later that their future proposals do not get committee attention.

In addition to the policy goals of the chair, committee members must consider the policy preferences of the majority of their committee colleagues and their party caucus. For example, a staffer for a Republican woman who often supports moderate positions on social welfare issues maintained that she does not actively seek the support of Democrats for her proposals and often downplays their role when lobbying Republican colleagues because she knows she will get the support of Democrats but she must convince those with the power, Republican majority members, to support her proposals. Therefore, she tries to get business and conservative groups to sign on to the bill, and, when lobbying colleagues, she frames issues with Republican themes. For example, she describes a proposal to increase funding for the Women, Infants, and Children Nutrition program as prevention, which will decrease health care costs.

The need to develop support among party colleagues often means that a legislator has to cede some ground and accept less than his or her preferred outcome. For example, as a member of the Ways and Means Committee, Nancy Johnson (R-CT) played a key role in getting the Republicans to include child-support enforcement in the welfare reform package. In fact, Republicans used her bill, which was the Congressional

Caucus for Women's Issues' child-support bill, as the blueprint for their child-support provisions (Congressional Quarterly Press 1996a; Casey and Carroll 1998). Yet Johnson recognized that many of her Republican colleagues disagreed about how far-reaching the child-support provisions should be because they feared too much government intrusion. Therefore, when Barbara Kennelly (D-CT) offered an amendment during committee markup that required states to adopt laws authorizing the suspension of professional, recreational, and drivers' licenses of parents who refused to pay their child support, Johnson voted against it, citing the fact that the welfare legislation included 90 percent of her bill and all of the most necessary provisions for child-support enforcement. The Kennelly provision was not essential and since some of the members on her side of the aisle opposed the requirement as a mandate on the states, she would not vote for the amendment.

Ensuing legislative battles later forced Republican Party leaders to include this provision in the bill because they feared Democratic efforts to portray them as antifamily would hurt the party in the 1996 elections. Republicans assigned the task of offering the amendment to Marge Roukema (R-NJ), a member of another committee with jurisdiction over welfare reform, instead of Johnson, because they did not want to draw attention to the fact that the Republicans on Ways and Means had voted against it. Although Johnson had voted against the amendment in committee, she voted for it on the floor and was one of the first members to speak in favor of the amendment during floor debate.[13]

What If a Woman Chaired the Committee or the Subcommittee?

Given the tremendous power over policy that committee and subcommittee chairs wield, such as their authority to schedule a markup for a bill and determine the scope of the legislative vehicle that is debated, a congresswoman's ascension to committee or subcommittee chair could make the committee agenda more open to women's issues. During the 103rd and 104th Congresses, no women chaired any of the committees or subcommittees with jurisdiction over a large amount of women's issue legislation.[14] However, one Republican congresswoman, Marge Roukema (R-NJ), served as the ranking member on the Labor-Management Relations Subcommittee of the Education and Labor Committee in the 103rd Congress. As ranking member, Roukema actively participated in the Clinton health reform debate and is widely credited as being a major force behind the passage of the Family and Medical Leave Act (Duncan and Lawrence 1995).

In the 106th Congress, Nancy Johnson (R-CT) became chair of the Ways and Means Human Resources Subcommittee, the subcommittee that had the major responsibility for welfare reform during the 104th Congress. Comparing the leadership style and priorities of Johnson and the former chair, moderate Republican Clay Shaw (R-FL), a staffer explained that Johnson is closer to Democratic groups like the children's advocates and the women's groups than Shaw was and therefore is more willing to give them a platform. For example, Shaw had refused to hold a hearing on child care because he said that he would not give the Democrats a forum, especially when the president (Bill Clinton) already has a huge media and publicity advantage. However, Johnson held a hearing on child care because she has a child-care background and she works with people inside and outside of Congress who care about this issue. She believes that Republicans need to build a record of examining the issue and listening to the relevant arguments so the party can justify the choices it makes.

While committee and subcommittee chairs can utilize hearings to galvanize attention for an issue and they control the legislative markup process, chairs still cannot pursue policy goals that will not be accepted by a majority of the party caucus and will antagonize important party constituencies. Thus, during a hearing on teen pregnancy, when Johnson argued with a representative from the Heritage Foundation, a conservative think tank, about the merits of the abstinence grant that was included in the welfare reform bill, she was blasted the next day in articles in conservative papers. As a staffer at the hearing explained, "Johnson wants programs that teach about abstinence and birth control to have access to the abstinence grant money. However, this program is a priority of social conservatives so she could never change it except maybe under cover of darkness and the social conservatives would have a fit and would run to Hastert and Armey [the party leaders]." Thus, regardless of gender, committee leaders, like all legislators, are constrained by their party's goals and must pursue their preferences on women's issues within the boundaries of what their party will accept.

Conclusion

The status of the committees as the central locus of policy development makes the identity of committee members an important influence on the content of policy outcomes. The regression models indicate that congresswomen are more likely to use their committee positions to advocate for women's issues. In addition, both Republican and Democratic women are more likely to offer feminist amendments than are their male colleagues. However, the importance of gender to the decision to sponsor social welfare amendments is largely overwhelmed by party affiliation, district characteristics, and committee position.

The small number of women in Congress and their even smaller representation on key committees and subcommittees limits the policy influence of women. Women's lack of institutional clout makes it difficult to draw firm conclusions about their potential impact during committee consideration of women's issue policies. This is particularly true in the case of Republican women. However, the regression analysis and anecdotal evidence concerning the commitment of Republican and Democratic women to the pursuit of gender-related causes indicates that including more women on key committees and subcommittees would likely result in the inclusion of more women's issue proposals, particularly feminist proposals, in committee legislation.

Chapter 6

Fighting for Women's Issues
on the Floor

The House floor represents the most public battleground in the policy-
making process. Legislators' statements on the floor are printed in the
Congressional Record and broadcast on C-SPAN and perhaps the national and local news for important interest groups and constituents
to judge. For those policies that survive the committee process to be
debated on the House floor, majority party leaders cooperate with the
committee and subcommittee chairs to structure choices and control
the policy outcomes. Meanwhile, the minority does what it can to influence policy or, alternatively, to offer amendments that will divide
the majority party and force their members to take embarrassing positions. An analysis of women's issue floor amendments reveals that the
highly constrained procedural rules that govern the House floor make
it difficult for male and female representatives who are not committee members to offer policy-altering amendments. However, the public
nature of the floor debate encourages the parties to recruit women to
speak as symbols of moral authority on women's issues.

Understanding Floor Participation

To facilitate majority party control over policy outcomes, all bills that
are debated on the floor are governed by a rule that specifies the length
of time for debate and the number and order of amendments that
can be offered. The Rules Committee, an arm of the party leadership,
hands down these guidelines. The majority party members of the Rules
Committee are appointed by the Speaker of the House. When a bill is
particularly controversial or complex, the committee may grant a modified closed or a closed rule that either prohibits amendments entirely
or allows the minority party to offer only one substitute amendment
and/or one motion to recommit the bill back to the committee process.

For example, during the 104th Congress, the House debated the Republican plan to overhaul Medicare, the Medicare Preservation Act (HR 2425), under a modified closed rule. Although many Democrats coveted the opportunity to offer amendments to reverse Republican Medicare budget cuts or to expand Medicare services, Republican leaders, anxious to keep their carefully crafted bill intact, granted a rule that only allowed a substitute amendment offered by the relevant committee's ranking minority member and a motion to recommit the bill by the Democratic minority leader (Congressional Quarterly Press 1996a). Thus, as the Medicare debate shows, even if a member wants to offer a women's issue amendment, he or she can be prevented by a restrictive rule.

Even without a restrictive rule, few members generally exercise their right to amend legislation on the floor. In his study of legislative participation, Hall (1996) found that even under an open rule where anyone can offer an amendment, on average, only 5 percent of members participate in amending activity and only 15 percent of members participate in floor debate or make insertions into the Congressional Record. Research indicates that the committee and subcommittee chairs and ranking members are the most active participants in floor deliberations. These members generally act as the bill managers who lead debate and allocate floor time to other members who want to speak on an issue. As bill managers, the majority party subcommittee and committee chairs command important procedural prerogatives, including consultation with the party leadership on the type of rule granted as well as rights of recognition that allow the chairs to be the first members recognized to offer amendments on behalf of the committee and the first to offer second-degree amendments or alternative amendments to limit the damage of unfriendly proposals to the committee bill. Beyond the committee leaders, subcommittee members are the most active floor participants, followed by other committee members and members of panels with related jurisdictions. Among the parties, minority party members are the most active floor amendment sponsors because they are generally the most dissatisfied with the legislation (Smith 1989; Hall 1996; Oleszek 1996). The important advantages held by majority party members and committee leaders highlight the need to pay close attention to institutional position when examining floor amending behavior.

To date, few studies examine gender differences in floor amending activity on women's issues. Research indicates that women are particularly engaged in floor activity concerning reproductive rights. For example, in the 103rd Congress, women led the fight to repeal the Hyde Amendment, which prohibits the use of Medicaid funds for abortions except in cases of rape, incest, or protection of the life of the mother (Dodson et al. 1995; Bingham 1997; Dodson 2000; Levy, Tien, and Aved 2002). In their studies of the Republican Welfare Reform Bill, Casey and Carroll (1998) and Norton (2002) found that Republican women worked to moderate the welfare bill by offering amendments on such feminist issues as child-support enforcement and child-care funding. However, Norton (1994, 1995, 1999, 2002) found that the ability of women to influence reproductive policy on the floor is limited by their lack of access to important committee positions. In her analysis of reproductive policy making from 1969 to 1992, Norton reports that committee and subcommittee members offered the majority of repro-ductive policy floor amendments and they were able to block policy changes supported by the majority of House members. Additionally, between 1989 and 1992, rank-and-file members who were not mem-bers of the relevant committee or a related panel with jurisdiction over other reproductive policies sponsored only 7 percent of reproductive floor amendments. Six pro-life congressmen sponsored almost all of the amendments offered by non–committee members.

This chapter moves beyond studies of individual bills and policy areas to evaluate gender differences in floor amending behavior on a range of women's issues. It focuses on institutional position to indicate whether congresswomen are more likely to offer women's issue amendments after accounting for the two most important determinants of floor par-ticipation: committee position and party affiliation.

Identifying Women's Issue Floor Amendments

The analysis of floor amending behavior is based on those women's is-sue bills that came to a vote on the House floor. Only about 10 percent of the more than five hundred women's issue initiatives proposed in each Congress were debated on the floor, fifty-one bills in the 103rd Congress and sixty-one bills in the 104th Congress. As with the anal-ysis of committee amendments, I reviewed the content of each floor amendment and included in my sample only those amendments that concerned women's issues. The final sample includes 227 amendments offered by 101 members in the 103rd Congress and 246 amendments proposed by 130 members in the 104th Congress.[1] Thus, fewer than one-third of the members serving in each Congress tried to change the direction of policies by offering an amendment on the floor.

The opportunities to offer gender-related amendments depend on the nature of the issues on the congressional agenda and the decisions made by the majority party concerning which bills to bring to the floor

Table 14   Women's Issue Bills by Rule Type and Number of Amendments

Rule Type	103rd Congress		104th Congress	
	No. of Bills	No. of Amendments	No. of Bills	No. of Amendments
Open	2	52	14	118
Modified open	10	95	7	24
Modified closed	0	0	15	77
Closed	0	0	2	4
Suspension				
of the rules	32	54	20	23
Voice vote	3	3	3	0
Privileged	4	23	0	0
Total bills/				
amendments	51	227	61	246

for a vote and the type of rule that will guide floor debate. Thus, in the 104th Congress, many Democrats and some Republicans coveted the opportunity to alter the Republican plans to overhaul Medicare and to reform health insurance practices by requiring the portability of health insurance when an individual changes jobs. However, both bills were debated under modified closed rules that strictly limited the number of amendments offered.

Table 14 groups the bills by the rule assigned and indicates the total number of amendments offered to bills in each rule category. As one moves from the open rules to the modified closed and closed rules, the additional restrictions specify which sections of a bill can be amended, the number of amendments that can be offered, and sometimes which individual members are allowed to offer the amendment. Among the other categories, bills passed under suspension of the rules cannot be substantively amended on the floor, but members can offer procedural amendments to these bills. Bills passed under suspension of the rules require a two-thirds House majority to pass.[2] By the time these bills reach the floor, they are generally noncontroversial, and they pass with a motion to suspend the rules that is usually offered by the committee or subcommittee chair.

As shown in table 14, legislators take advantage of the opportunity to offer amendments when legislation is debated under more open rules. Thus, in the 103rd Congress, education issues attracted the most amendments, fifty-one, because the bill reauthorizing the Elementary and Secondary Education Act (ESEA) was debated under an open rule. This bill dealt with a large portion of federal education programs including the Title I program for disadvantaged students, the Eisenhower Math and

Science grants, bilingual education, and the Women's Educational Equity Act. The bill also attracted numerous social policy riders, such as amendments restricting sex education, banning the distribution of condoms in school, requiring school prayer, and regulating school violence. Similarly, issues related to welfare reform and health care constituted the majority of amendments proposed in the 104th Congress because a low-income housing bill and the two appropriations bills funding programs administered by the Department of Labor, Health and Human Services, and Education were debated under open rules. (See app. B for a complete list of the women's issue bills considered on the House floor, the rule assigned, and the number of amendments offered to each bill.)

Finally, those members who decide to participate in the floor debate can offer three types of amendments: first-degree, second-degree, and procedural amendments. First- and second-degree amendments are substantive amendments that seek to change the content of a bill. For example, a legislator may offer a first-degree amendment that increases funding for Head Start or requires health insurance companies to cover a forty-eight-hour stay after childbirth. A second-degree amendment seeks to alter the first-degree amendment in some way.

Procedural amendments utilize House rules to achieve policy goals. They can be amendments to move the process along, such as motions to suspend the rules and pass the bill, or motions to go to a conference committee with the Senate.[3] Representatives often use procedural amendments to achieve substantive policy changes. For example, members raise points of order to declare that an amendment is not germane to the bill and should be ruled out of order. Legislators also employ procedural amendments to delay or disrupt the floor debate to gain attention to their cause and possibly derail a bill. For example, during the 103rd Congress, Congressman Christopher Smith (R-NJ) led a last minute attempt by pro-life members to derail the Freedom of Access to Abortion Clinic Entrances bill. On a routine motion to go to conference, Smith and his allies forced seven separate roll-call votes and tried to kill the legislation by offering amendments to table the bill and to send the bill back to committee (Congressional Quarterly Press 1995a).

Advocating for Women's Issues on the Floor

Despite the highly structured nature of the floor debate in which party and committee leaders dictate how many amendments are permitted and who can participate in the debate, do congresswomen distinguish

Table 15   The 103rd and 104th Congresses: Women's Issue Floor Amendment Sponsorship

	Democratic				Republican			
	Men (103rd $N = 222$; 104th $N = 165$)		Women (103rd $N = 36$; 104th $N = 31$)		Men (103rd $N = 163$; 104th $N = 217$)		Women (103rd $N = 12$; 104th $N = 17$)	
	Sponsor (%)	Ams.	Sponsor (%)	Ams.	Sponsor (%)	Ams.	Sponsor (%)	Ams.
103rd Congress	19	101	28	22	28	98	25	5
104th Congress	30	89	42	29	29	121	35	7

NOTE: *N* represents the number of members in the category. Thus, 222 Democratic men served in the 103rd Congress. Ams. = Amendments.

themselves as more active advocates for women's interests on the floor? Table 15 displays the number of women's issue floor amendments sponsored by Democratic and Republican men and women. Too few members sponsored feminist and antifeminist floor amendments to justify a separate analysis of floor amendments by policy area.[4]

Table 15 demonstrates that Republican and Democratic women reacted differently to minority party status. It appears that in the 103rd Congress, Republican women were less active sponsors of women's issue floor amendments than were Republican men, indicating that these women may have been less dissatisfied with Democratic proposals on women's issues than were their male colleagues. Conversely, when Democratic women were relegated to minority status in the 104th Congress, they opposed Republican initiatives on women's issues even more aggressively than did Democratic men.

As members of the majority, it appears that majority party congresswomen are always more likely to offer women's issue floor amendments than are their male colleagues. Thus, in both Congresses, almost 10 percent more majority party women, Democrats in the 103rd Congress and Republicans in the 104th Congress, proposed women's issue amendments than majority party men did. These majority party gender differences may reflect a deeper commitment to women's issues that compels congresswomen to seek the inclusion of these interests on the floor. Alternatively, women's lack of seniority may make floor amending a more necessary strategy to gain attention to women's issues. Since women generally do not hold committee and subcommittee chairmanships and senior positions on the committees, it is more difficult for them to influence the policy content of the committee bill. The regression analyses in the next section account for the important influences of committee position and majority/minority membership on a legislator's decision to offer amendments on the floor.

Modeling Gender Differences in Floor Amending Behavior

The ordered logit models in table 16 demonstrate that institutional position is the most important predictor of which legislators will offer women's issue amendments. The procedural advantages held by the committee and subcommittee leaders in their role as bill managers make them the most likely members to offer women's issue amendments. Among the rank and file, those legislators with a seat on a women's issue subcommittee have the most knowledge about the bill and their informed staff can draft amendments more easily than staffers for members outside of the subcommittee.[5]

In addition to committee position, minority party membership is an important predictor of women's issue floor amending behavior. In the 103rd Congress, minority party conservative Republican men were more likely to offer women's issue floor amendments than Democrats were. In the 104th Congress, the ideology score indicates that minority party liberal Democrats were the most likely to offer women's issue floor amendments, while their conservative Democratic colleagues were less likely to offer these amendments than moderate Republicans were. Given their control of the committee process and the rules governing floor debate, majority party members are usually the most satisfied with the product coming out of the committee and therefore feel less compelled to modify the bill on the House floor. In contrast, minority party members whose policy proposals have often already been rejected in committee will try to gain support for their amendments one last time in front of the full chamber. When passage is unlikely, minority members will use their amendments to make policy statements that they can use in the next election to justify their reelection and the need for the electorate to award their party majority status.

Since floor action represents the final showdown between the agendas of the two parties, I included variables measuring the influence of minority and majority leaders in the floor amendment models. These dummy variables account for the majority/minority leader, whips, and conference chairs in each party.[6] While the party leadership variables are positive and bordering on significance in the 103rd Congress, they are entirely insignificant predictors of women's issue floor amending in the 104th Congress. This result may reflect the fact that during a large portion of the 104th Congress, the leaders concentrated their attention

Table 16   The 103rd and 104th Congresses: Floor Amendment Ordered Logit Models

Independent Variables	All Floor Amendments	
	103rd Congress	104th Congress
Republican women	−.505	1.56[+]
	(−.57)	(1.9)
Democratic women	.843[+]	.871*
	(1.76)	(2.03)
Republican men	−.344	1.23[+]
	(−.53)	(−1.72)
Ideology	1.22[+]	−1.19[+]
	(1.73)	(−1.84)
Freshman	−.537[+]	−.938**
	(−1.69)	(−2.76)
Southern	−.086	−.154
	(−.26)	(−.51)
% Hispanic	−1.89	−.892
	(−1.51)	(−.95)
% Urban	1.77*	.503
	(2.04)	(.65)
% Black	−.736	−2.46*
	(−.62)	(−2.33)
Median household income	.11	−.058
	(.55)	(−.3)
Woman's subcommittee	.744***	.829***
	(3.52)	(3.25)
Woman's subcommittee chair	4.33***	2.01**
	(3.79)	(2.59)
Woman's subcommittee ranking member	3.04**	1.78*
	(2.56)	(2.25)
Woman's committee chair	3.96***	1.95[+]
	(3.28)	(1.94)
Woman's committee ranking member	.522	2.14*
	(.39)	(2.49)
Majority leader	1.57	No amendments
	(1.56)	sponsored
Minority leader	2.46[+]	.343
	(1.83)	(.27)
Number of observations	432	429
% Correct	79	72
PRE statistic (%)	9	8
PRE ± 1 (%)	17	20

NOTE: Numbers in parentheses are Z-statistics (coefficients/standard errors). "No amendments sponsored" indicates that none of the members in the category sponsored an amendment; therefore, since there is no variation in the data, a coefficient cannot be estimated.

[+] $p \leq .1$.

* $p \leq .05$.

** $p \leq .01$.

*** $p \leq .001$.

on passing or blocking the Contract with America. Outside of the welfare reform bill and some tax issues like the $500 per child tax credit, the ten-point Contract with America did not focus on women's issues.

Even after accounting for the overwhelming importance of a legislator's institutional position, the models in table 16 demonstrate that gender does exert an important influence on women's issue floor amending behavior, particularly for Democratic women. In both the 103rd and the 104th Congresses, Democratic women were among the most active proponents of women's interests on the floor. In fact, in both Congresses, being a Democratic woman is an even more important predictor of floor amending behavior than having a seat on one of the subcommittees that considered the most gender-related legislation. While one would expect minority party legislators to be the most aggressive proponents of amendments on the floor, in the 103rd Congress, majority party Democratic women were even more likely to offer women's issue amendments than minority party moderate Republican men. Thus, when Democratic women served in the majority they tried to incorporate additional gender-related concerns into Democratic initiatives. As minority party legislators, in the 104th Congress, Democratic women worked even more aggressively than Democratic men to combat conservative initiatives on women's issues.

Moreover, the amending behavior of Republican women does not conform to expectations based on majority/minority party status. The combination of ideology and party variables indicates that when Republicans ascended to the majority in the 104th Congress, moderate Republican men and women were more active proponents of women's issue amendments than were conservative Democratic men. This finding suggests that as members of the majority, Republican women wanted to moderate the conservative policies that their Republican colleagues brought to the floor, and these female ideological moderates were slightly more likely to engage in floor activity on women's issues than were their moderate male Republican colleagues.

Interview discussions also highlighted a shift in the legislative activity of Republican women when they gained the majority. One staffer to a liberal Democratic congressman noted that "moderate Republicans (male and female) are a hot commodity right now. They are heavily lobbied by interest groups that support Democrats because the groups need to reach to the right to show they have support. If Democrats get the majority back, conservative groups will court the conservative Democrats." Similarly, a moderate Republican congresswoman revealed that she works much harder as a member of the majority because "all the threatened agencies like Legal Services and the National Endowment for the Arts and all the women's interest groups come to me and ask me to rescue them and to speak to the leadership on their behalf." A staffer for another moderate Republican woman explained that "a lot of groups that would normally go to Democrats for support now come to her [the congresswoman] because she is in the majority and she is moderate. . . . As one of only five moderate Republicans on the committee and the only woman, a lot of Democratic groups come to her to get support for various women's issues." Thus, it appears that moderates, particularly moderate Republican women, are more supportive of liberal positions on women's issues than are their other Republican colleagues. The interest groups perceive these moderate women as more sympathetic to their issues and actively seek the support of these congresswomen for their causes.

What If There Were More Women in Positions of Strategic Influence?

The fact that women, particularly Democratic women, are still significantly more active sponsors of women's issue floor amendments even after accounting for committee position highlights the important question of whether these issues would receive more attention if there were more women on the relevant committees. As with the analysis of committee amendments in the previous chapter, I address this question by calculating predicted probabilities. The probabilities in figures 9 and 10 measure the likelihood that a representative with a given gender, party, ideology, and subcommittee seat will offer a women's issue amendment on the floor.[7]

As expected, in every case, legislators who sit on women's issue subcommittees were more likely to sponsor women's issue floor amendments than were those who do not hold seats on these subcommittees.[8] However, the graphs reveal important gender differences in the use of institutional power. In the 103rd Congress, majority party liberal and conservative Democratic women both on and off the women's issue subcommittees were more likely to sponsor women's issue floor amendments than were similarly situated Democratic men. This result indicates that Democratic women still wanted to change the majority party's committee bill to give more attention to women's issues or perhaps to incorporate even more liberal policy stands on women's issues than the committee would endorse. As members of the opposition party in the 104th Congress, Democratic women on and off the

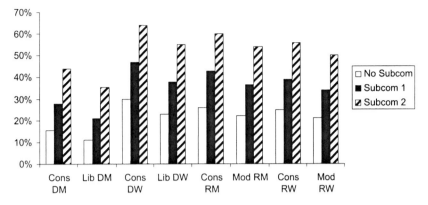

Figure 9   The 103rd Congress: Probability of Sponsoring a Women's Issue Floor Amendment

NOTE: *Cons* = conservative; *Lib* = liberal; *Mod* = moderate; *DM* = Democratic men; *DW* = Democratic women; *RM* = Republican men; and *RW* = Republican women. The bars represent the mean probability that a member with a given gender, party, ideology, and subcommittee seat will offer a women's issue amendment on the floor. To characterize members as hypothetical liberal or conservative Democrats and moderate or conservative Republicans, the ideology scores are set at the 25 percent and 75 percent quartiles within each party. In most cases, the subcommittee variable is coded 0 for those who are not on the relevant subcommittees and 1 for those members with a seat on the subcommittees. In this case, the subcommittee variable is divided into three values, 0, 1, and 2. Members with a seat on the Elementary, Secondary, and Vocational Education Subcommittee are assigned a value of 2 because the legislation considered by this subcommittee attracted an unusually high number of women's issue amendments during floor consideration in the 103rd Congress. See appendix A for more information on which subcommittees considered the most women's issue legislation.

women's issue subcommittees were comparatively the most active floor participants offering counteramendments to conservative Republican proposals on women's issues.

With regard to Republicans, figures 9 and 10 demonstrate that, as minority party legislators, Republican men and women were substantially equivalent in their efforts to amend Democratic policy proposals, with conservative men offering the most amendments. However, as majority party legislators, Republican women, particularly moderate Republican women, increased their amending activity. Thus, in the 104th Congress, moderate Republican women were much more likely to offer women's issue floor amendments than their male Republican counterparts were, and these women were just as likely to offer these amendments as liberal Democratic men. These results, along with the interview evidence, suggest that Republican women engaged in floor action to moderate the

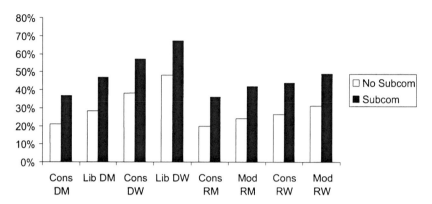

Figure 10   The 104th Congress: Probability of Sponsoring a Women's Issue Floor Amendment

NOTE: *Cons* = conservative; *Lib* = liberal; *Mod* = moderate; *DM* = Democratic men; *DW*= Democratic women; *RM* = Republican men; and *RW* = Republican women. The bars represent the mean probability that a member with a given gender, party, ideology, and subcommittee seat will offer a women's issue amendment on the floor. To characterize members as hypothetical liberal or conservative Democrats and moderate or conservative Republicans, the ideology scores are set at the 25 percent and 75 percent quartiles within each party.

conservative bills emerging from the committees and party leadership task forces.

The Case of Abortion

The debates over abortion in the 103rd and 104th Congresses highlight the interaction of individual policy interests, committee position, and majority/minority power. Since the Supreme Court's *Roe v. Wade* decision in the 1970s, the House floor has often provided the setting for major battles on the abortion issue. In both Congresses, legislators debated both free-standing bills on abortion, including the Freedom of Access to Abortion Clinic Entrances Act in the 103rd Congress and the Partial Birth Abortion Act in the 104th Congress and abortion proposals offered as legislative riders to appropriations bills. In fact, Republican changes to the House rules in the 104th Congress made it easier to offer these limitation amendments to appropriations bills, and abortion opponents took full advantage of these rules changes (Evans and Oleszceck 1997).

In the 103rd Congress, feminist, pro-choice floor amendments were largely offered by Democratic women and male committee and subcommittee chairs trying to protect their bills from pro-life attacks. In contrast, Republican men, both committee and non–committee members, offered all of the antifeminist, pro-life abortion amendments. The debate over the Hyde amendment concerning Medicaid funding of abortions exemplifies the dynamics of the abortion debate in the 103rd Congress. The three women serving on the Labor, Health and Human Services, and Education Subcommittee led the fight to strike the Hyde Amendment during the subcommittee markup. However, the pro-life Democratic chairman of the Appropriations Committee reattached the amendment during the full committee markup. When the legislation reached the floor, Pat Schroeder (D-CO), a non–committee member who cochaired the Congressional Caucus for Women's Issues, offered a motion to strike the amendment as legislating on an appropriations bill. However, with the assistance of the pro-life, Democratic Appropriations Committee chair, minority Republican Congressman Henry Hyde (R-IL) was able to use procedural maneuvers to reattach the amendment. In the end, the Hyde Amendment prevailed with two new exceptions allowing Medicaid funding in situations of rape and incest or when the life of the mother is endangered (Norton 1994, 1995, 1999, 2002; Dodson et al. 1995; Bingham 1997; Dodson 2000).

Since Republicans gained the majority, Democratic women and Democratic men, particularly the committee and subcommittee ranking members, continued to offer feminist pro-choice amendments on the floor. These Democrats were now joined by moderate Republican women and men, both committee and non–committee members, who tried to moderate the conservative bills coming out of the committees. Male Republicans utilized their new committee leadership posts and their positions as majority party members on and off the committees to offer all but one of the antifeminist, pro-life floor amendments. A conservative Democratic congressman offered the other pro-life amendment. This pattern continues in the current Republican-controlled Congress.

A moderate Republican congressman explained the new institutional dynamic. As an advocate of family planning, he recently worked with Nancy Pelosi (D-CA), the Democratic ranking minority member of the Appropriations Committee's Foreign Operations Subcommittee, to draft an amendment to reverse a pro-life proposal to reinstate the Mexico City Policy, which prohibits funding to international family planning organizations that perform abortions or engage in lobbying in favor of abortion.[9] Three days before the House considered the bill, he was told that the Rules Committee would not make his amendment in order, meaning he would not be allowed to offer the amendment from the floor. He then spent the entire day with the Speaker's chief of staff negotiating a deal to get his amendment made in order. As a member of the majority, he had the power and the access to leadership to negotiate for his amendment. A Democrat could not get this access; if he told the leaders it was Pelosi's amendment they would not make it in order. If the situation was reversed and Democrats controlled the majority, Pelosi would have to take the lead and lobby her party leadership.

These reproductive policy examples demonstrate that Democratic women remained equally active and committed to women's issues across both Congresses. However, the Republican ascendancy to the majority required Republican legislators who favored more liberal positions on women's issues to utilize their majority power by taking a more aggressive role in floor debate and by offering amendments to moderate conservative Republican legislative initiatives. This new institutional dynamic forced moderate Republicans to take a more aggressive and public stand against the wishes of the majority of their party colleagues, thus increasing the cost of being a pro-choice Republican. Consequently, the congressman quoted above asserted "it was a lot easier when we were just expected to bring along our contingent of [pro-choice] votes."

Representing Women in Floor Debate

In addition to providing an opportunity to alter the policy content of legislation, the floor debate gives legislators a forum to express their views on a bill and to lobby colleagues to accept their positions. Representatives often point to personal experiences to demonstrate their expertise on an issue and to bolster their credibility with colleagues. Thus, congresswomen often point to their experiences as women and as mothers when speaking on a variety of women's issues (Cramer Walsh 2002; Levy, Tien and Aved 2002). For example, in a floor speech calling on members to support the 1993 Family and Medical Leave Act, Marge Roukema (R-NJ) pointed to her experience caring for her son who was dying with leukemia. During the debate over the welfare reform bill, Lynn Woolsey (D-CA) asserted that she "differ(s) from every other member of this House because [she is] the only member of Congress to have been a welfare mother. So [her] opinions are not based on theory. They are based on real-life experience" (Duncan and Lawrence 1995). Similarly, a staffer for a Democratic congresswoman said that in order to establish her moral authority, "When a bill deals with children's issues she starts off by saying 'as a mother.' When a bill deals with gay rights, she says 'as a Catholic and a mother of five.'" Another Republican staff member explained that her boss speaks for pro-life causes because "people assume that all women are pro-choice, but she can say I am a woman and I am pro-life and she is automatically seen as having expertise. It is just like when the doctors speak on Medicare and health reform. They can say that I went through this from personal experience and I can tell you what the ramifications of the policy are."

Any natural interest that congresswomen have in acting as advocates for women's issues is magnified by the fact that bill sponsors and party leaders actively seek their support as experts and symbols of moral authority on an issue. As one Democratic staffer stated, speakers are chosen for "credibility and dramatic effect." This strategic deployment of women is most evident in the numerous floor debates on abortion. In a typical example, a Republican staffer maintained that when the congressman offered his amendment against FDA approval of the "morning-after pill," RU 486, he looked for "speakers with a scientific background, other doctors like Weldon [(R-FL)] and he asked women because the Democrats are always putting out their pro-choice women." Staff members for both pro-choice and pro-life Republican women claimed that interest groups constantly called their offices asking them to speak on the abortion issue. A staffer to one of the more active pro-life women explained: "There are only six pro-life women and a lot of pro-life votes. The congresswoman has taken more responsibility on the issue than she wanted. She believes in the issue but she does not actively seek opportunities to work on it. She does not have to because they always come to her. Many of the pro-life women do not want to be tagged with it as their only issue, and it would be if they answered all the requests to speak on it." Thus, the natural interest that these pro-life women have in the abortion issue is compounded by pro-life interest groups and male colleagues who want these women to lend credibility and moral authority to their cause.

Conclusion

Analysis of floor amending behavior shows that institutional factors—particularly a member's committee position and status as a member of the majority or minority party—limit a representative's ability to offer floor amendments on women's issues. Subcommittee members command the most knowledge about a bill and are more readily able to formulate amendments, while committee and subcommittee chairs utilize their procedural prerogatives to protect their bills from unwelcome changes. Minority party legislators are often the most dissatisfied with the version of the bill that the majority has placed on the floor, and they will use the floor debate as a final opportunity to change the bill or to force the majority to vote on divisive amendments. When bills are debated under restrictive rules, bill opponents must rely on sympathetic majority party representatives to carry their cause to the floor.

Even in the highly constrained atmosphere of the House floor, Democratic women were the most active advocates for women's interests on the floor. As majority party representatives, these women offered amendments to increase attention to women's issues, to encourage the House to accept more liberal positions on issues like abortion, and to counter conservative proposals. In the 104th Congress, Democratic women used the floor debate to vehemently oppose Republican initiatives on welfare, health care, and abortion. Unlike their conservative colleagues, who offered more women's issue amendments when their party was in the minority, moderate Republican women increased their amending activity on women's issues when their party gained majority status. Interviews suggest that moderate Republican women, along with some moderate Republican congressmen, acted to soften the conservative women's issue initiatives put forth by their party. This desire to moderate leadership bills was reinforced by the lobbying efforts of women's groups and other liberal interests who viewed the moderate Republican women as their last hope in combating the initiatives of a majority party opposed to their favored causes.

Finally, female representatives speak distinctively in Congress. In floor speeches to gain support for an amendment or to promote their position on the overall bill, congresswomen often point to their experiences as women or as mothers to gain credibility on an issue. Other players in the political process take advantage of this experience. Political parties, interest groups, and sponsors of particular bills seek out female representatives to speak as symbols of moral authority on various women's issues.

Chapter 7

Roll-Call Voting:
Taking a Public Position
on Women's Issues

From 1990 to 1997, Congresswoman Susan Molinari maintained a largely pro-choice voting record while representing a majority pro-life, Italian, Catholic, suburban district in Staten Island, N.Y. Although Molinari generally won reelection by a wide margin, her pro-choice stand did not come without political costs. In her congressional memoir, Molinari explains that the Right to Life Party always fielded a female candidate to oppose her in the election. In every campaign, protesters screaming "murderer" followed her to conventions, fundraisers, and speaking engagements, and for years, on almost every Saturday afternoon, pro-life activists picketed her Staten Island office "waving photographs of aborted fetuses" (Molinari 1998).

While most votes do not inspire this level of action among constituents and interest groups, members of Congress recognize that a single vote potentially has the power to make or break their careers. Groups from both ends of the ideological spectrum carefully scrutinize members' voting records and distribute voter guides to inform constituents about where their representative stands on issues ranging from labor and business concerns to environmental protection. Additionally, election opponents scour a legislator's record to exploit inconsistencies that can turn the tide in their favor. Thus, in the 2000 Democratic presidential primary, Bill Bradley used Vice President Al Gore's votes in the House of Representatives from 1979 to paint him as a social conservative on race relations, abortion rights, and gun control (Marks 2000). In this chapter I examine whether, despite high levels of public scrutiny and partisan pressure, congresswomen will be more likely to vote in favor of liberal positions on women's issues than will their male colleagues. I also evaluate whether the importance of gender varies with how directly a vote can be linked to consequences for women as a group.

Deciding How to Vote

Political scientists have conducted extensive research on congressional roll-call voting behavior. Much of this research points to the overwhelming influence of ideology, partisanship, and constituency factors as the determinants of representatives' voting decisions. For example, Kingdon (1989) found that the views of other legislators and the interests of the constituency are the most important influences on a member's voting behavior. Representatives look to colleagues with similar ideological viewpoints and expertise on the issue, while constituency characteristics act as constraints limiting the range of acceptable choices. When examining the specific content of legislation, some researchers claim that voting alignments vary across policy areas such as foreign policy/ defense and social welfare issues (Clausen 1973; Wilcox and Clausen 1991). However, others reject the need for multiple dimensions and assert that a single liberal-conservative dimension explains at least 80 percent of the variance in roll-call voting (Poole and Daniels 1985; Poole 1988; Poole and Rosenthal 1991, 1997; McCarty, Poole, and Rosenthal 1997). Generally, the major roll-call vote studies do not consider how social identities such as race and gender affect a representative's voting record.

Most of the studies that focus directly on how gender influences members' roll-call vote decisions investigate whether congresswomen are more liberal than their male colleagues, rather than asking whether women vote together on women's issues. Since there is no reason to believe that women will always vote more liberally than men across the policy spectrum, the results of these studies have been mixed (Frankovic 1977; Gehlen 1977; Leader 1977; Welch 1985; Burrell 1994; Vega and Firestone 1995; Clark 1998). For example, Frankovic (1977) found significant gender differences in male and female representatives' voting patterns. However, she could not determine if these differences were due to the impact of gender or to the fact that women were more likely than men to represent urban districts and districts with a large percentage of minorities. Analyzing conservative coalition support scores, for the 93rd–96th (1973–80) Congresses and the 100th–102nd (1987–92) Congress respectively, Welch (1985) and Burrell (1994) found that, while party is the most significant predictor of a liberal voting record, congresswomen are more liberal than their male colleagues within the same party. This is especially true among Republicans and Southern Democrats. Conversely, McCarty, Poole, and Rosenthal (1997) maintain that gender and race are two issue areas that could disturb the

unidimensional, liberal-conservative voting patterns that have traditionally prevailed in Congress. Yet they claim that the higher degree of
liberalism among congresswomen can be entirely explained by district
characteristics.

While so many studies examine the contribution of gender to a representative's overall ideology, few have tried to discern the impact of
gender on support for liberal positions on women's issues specifically.
Tatalovich and Schier (1993) and I (Swers 1998) found that gender is a
significant predictor of pro-choice voting. Furthermore, Burrell (1994),
Dolan (1997), and I (Swers 1998) found that congresswomen were more
likely than their male colleagues to support a set of women's issues
identified by women's interest groups. In this chapter, I examine the
impact of gender on women's issue roll-call voting in the two widely
varying political contexts of the 103rd and 104th Congresses. To further
evaluate whether the importance of gender varies with how directly an
issue affects women as a group, I also analyze the subset of women's
issue votes concerning reproductive policies. These reproductive policies represent perhaps the most frequently voted on women's issue from
the 1970s to the present.

Identifying Women's Issue Votes

To create a sample of women's issue votes, I employ the vote ratings of
the American Association of University Women (1994a, 1996a). I then
increased the sample size and range of women's issue votes by supple-
menting these votes with additional important roll-call votes identified by the Congressional Caucus for Women's Issues (1993, 1994) in
the 103rd Congress and Women's Policy, Inc. (1996; see also Clemmitt,
Primmer, and Simms 1997), in the 104th Congress.[1] The final women's
issue vote samples include fourteen votes in the 103rd Congress and
fifteen votes in the 104th Congress.

The samples measure voting on a wide range of women's issues
including education, women's health, welfare, and violence against
women. For example, the fourteen-vote sample for the 103rd Congress
incorporates three votes on education issues, including votes on President Clinton's National Service Program and the bill reauthorizing the
major federal education program, the Elementary and Secondary Education Act.[2] Members of the 103rd Congress also cast six votes concerning women's health, including the Hyde amendment, which restricted
Medicaid funding of abortion; the National Institutes of Health (NIH)

Revitalization Act, which encompassed programs for a range of women's health issues; and the Freedom of Access to (Abortion) Clinic Entrances Act (FACE). Other bills incorporated in the sample include two votes on issues related to violence against women and votes concerning family and medical leave, federal nutrition programs, and the creation of an Office of Women's Business Ownership.

The fifteen-vote sample for the 104th Congress incorporates three votes on education issues; a vote on the appropriations bill funding the programs of the Departments of Labor, Health and Human Services, and Education, an effort to raise the minimum wage; and two votes on welfare reform, including the final welfare reform bill, the Personal Responsibility Act of 1996.[3] Members also cast two votes concerning gay rights, including the Defense of Marriage Act, which was designed to prevent gay marriages, and six votes on issues concerning women's reproductive health, including the Partial Birth Abortion Act and efforts to eliminate the funding of international family planning programs.

Creating the Women's Issue Vote Support Score

To determine whether congresswomen are more likely to take liberal positions on women's issue votes than are their male colleagues, I calculated the number of times each legislator supported the liberal position on a women's issue bill. For example, in the 103rd Congress, a member who voted for the Family and Medical Leave Act and against the Hyde Amendment to restrict Medicaid funding of abortions received a score of one for each bill. I then created a women's issue support score by taking the sum of each representative's votes and dividing them by the number of women's issue votes he or she cast. Thus, in the 103rd Congress, a member who voted in a liberal direction on seven women's issue bills and cast a vote on thirteen of the fourteen bills received a score of 54 percent.[4]

The previous chapters demonstrate that through all stages of the legislative process, gender exerts the strongest influence on the decision to support and advocate feminist legislation. On the House floor, the most frequently debated feminist issue is reproductive rights. Therefore, I also analyzed a reproductive issue support score that includes five bills in the 103rd Congress and six bills in the 104th Congress.

The five bills making up the reproductive issues score for the 103rd Congress include the Family Planning Amendments Act of 1993; the Hyde Amendment concerning federal funding of abortion to the Fiscal Year 1995 Labor, Health and Human Services, and Education

Appropriations Bill; the Unsoeld Amendment on sex education to the ESEA; the National Institutes of Health (NIH) Revitalization Act, which included provisions on a wide range of women's health issues from breast cancer to contraception; and the Freedom of Access to (Abortion) Clinic Entrances Act (FACE).

During the 104th Congress, the Republican leadership attached numerous social policy riders to the appropriations bills that fund government programs in an effort to force President Clinton to accept conservative initiatives that he would veto if they were presented as stand-alone legislation. Therefore, the battle over reproductive rights was largely conducted through dueling amendments offered to various appropriations bills. The six votes constituting the reproductive issues score for the 104th Congress include the Lowey Amendment to the Fiscal Year 1996 Omnibus Appropriations Bill, concerning allowing Medicaid funding for abortion; the Greenwood Amendment restoring domestic family planning funding to the Fiscal Year 1996 Labor, Health and Human Services, and Education Appropriations Bill; the DeLauro Amendment to the Department of Defense Reauthorization Act of 1995 regarding the lifting of the ban on the use of private funds for abortions at military hospitals; the Partial Birth Abortion Ban Act of 1995; the Lowey Amendment to the Fiscal Year 1997 Labor, Health and Human Services, and Education Bill, concerning striking the ban on funding for embryo research; and the Smith Amendment to the Fiscal Year 1996 Foreign Operations Appropriation Bill, concerning the restriction of international family planning funding.

Comparing Gender Differences in Voting Behavior

Tables 17 and 18 provide an overview of the women's issue and reproductive roll-call voting data. Naturally, party appears to be the most important indicator of liberal voting on women's issues and the subset of reproductive issues. Across both Congresses, Democratic women are the most active supporters of liberal positions on women's issues, voting liberally on an average of thirteen of the fourteen women's issue votes in the 103rd Congress and 13.5 of the fifteen women's issue votes in the 104th Congress. However, Democratic men are also highly supportive of liberal positions on women's issues. Across the two Congresses, Republican women register the most dramatic change in their women's issue voting behavior. When Republicans gained the majority in the 104th Congress, support for liberal positions on women's issue votes among Republican men dropped an average of 26 percent.

Table 17 The 103rd Congress: All Women's Issue and Reproductive Issue Votes

Representative/ Issue Area	Mean	Standard Deviation	Minimum	Maximum
Democratic:				
Men ($N = 221$):				
All women's	11.8	2	6	14
Reproductive	3.8	1.4	0	5
Women ($N = 35$):				
All women's	13	.9	11	14
Reproductive	4.7	.7	3	5
Republican:				
Men ($N = 163$):				
All women's	5.3	3.3	1	14
Reproductive	1	1.5	0	5
Women ($N = 12$):				
All women's	10.2	3.5	2	14
Reproductive	3.7	1.7	0	5

NOTE: N = Number of members in the category. There are 221 male Democrats rather than 222 and 35 female Democrats rather than 36 included in the roll-call vote analysis because William Natcher (D-KY), chair of the Appropriations Committee and the Labor, Health and Human Services, and Education Subcommittee, died midsession and Eleanor Holmes Norton (D = DC), the delegate from Washington, D.C., cannot vote.

Table 18 The 104th Congress: All Women's Issue and Reproductive Issue Votes

Representative/ Issue Area	Mean	Standard Deviation	Minimum	Maximum
Democratic:				
Men ($N = 165$):				
All women's	11.2	3.4	2	15
Reproductive	4.2	2.3	0	6
Women ($N = 30$):				
All women's	13.5	1.8	8	15
Reproductive	5.5	1	2	6
Republican:				
Men ($N = 217$):				
All women's	1.8	2.6	0	13
Reproductive	.8	1.7	0	6
Women ($N = 17$):				
All women's	3.9	3.6	0	11
Reproductive	2.5	2.6	0	6

NOTE: N = Number of members in the category. There are 30 female Democrats rather than 31 because the delegate from Washington, D.C., Eleanor Holmes Norton, cannot vote.

However, Republican women reduced their support for liberal positions on women's issues by an average of almost 50 percent.[5]

This decline in liberal women's issue voting among Republican women is partially due to the influx of new conservative freshman congresswomen who voted for between zero and two bills. However, the veteran, moderate Republican women also reduced their liberal women's issue voting. For example, Susan Molinari, who became vice-chair of the Republican party caucus, voted for thirteen of the fourteen women's issue votes in the 103rd Congress and only five of the fifteen votes in the 104th Congress. Similarly, the longest serving Republican woman, Marge Roukema (R-NJ), voted for the liberal position on twelve of the fourteen votes in the 103rd Congress and only seven of the fifteen votes in the 104th Congress.

Uncovering the Impact of Gender on Women's Issue Voting

While the voting patterns displayed in tables 17 and 18 highlight the existence of gender differences in voting behavior on women's issues, research on roll-call voting emphasizes legislators' overwhelming concern with how their votes will be interpreted by district constituents in the next election (Kingdon 1989; Poole and Rosenthal 1997). This common preoccupation with reelection leaves little room for the impact of social identity. To make sure that gender differences in voting behavior do not actually reflect a pattern in which more women are elected from districts that support liberal representatives, as suggested by McCarty, Poole, and Rosenthal (1997), I created regression models that evaluate the impact of gender in the presence of the important ideological and constituency factors that guide the voting decisions of representatives.

Tables 19 and 20 utilize ordinary least squares regression models with White's correction for heteroskedasticity to evaluate the influence of gender on women's issue voting.[6] The regression results in table 19 demonstrate that even though ideology is by far the most important predictor of women's issue voting, the presence of a female representative does exert a significant impact on the voting decision. The importance of gender largely stems from the voting behavior of Republican women. In the 103rd Congress, the estimates indicate that the presence of a Republican woman increases the likelihood of liberal voting on women's issues by approximately 21 percent. At the same time, the extremely insignificant coefficient for Democratic women indicates that Democratic men are just as likely to cast liberal votes on women's issues as Democratic women are. However, when Republican women support

Table 19   The 103rd and 104th Congresses: OLS Regression Models on All Women's Issue Roll-Call Votes

Independent Variables	All Women's Issues	
	103rd Congress	104th Congress
Republican women	.205**	.13*
	(3.18)	(2.49)
Democratic women	−.005	.04*
	(−.243)	(2.05)
Republican men	−.027	.05
	(−.606)	(.97)
Ideology	−.57***	−.643***
	(−11.73)	(−13.61)
African-American representative	−.092	−.05
	(−1.53)	(−.94)
Religion	−.025	−.034*
	(−1.5)	(−2.33)
Freshman	.037*	.003
	(2.22)	(.22)
% Vote for Clinton	−.03	.351**
	(−.224)	(2.99)
% Vote for Perot	.176	.368*
	(1.02)	(2.14)
Southern	−.031+	.044*
	(−1.75)	(2.56)
% Black	.057	−.003
	(.518)	(−.03)
% Urban	−.022	.017
	(−.562)	(.44)
Median household income	.032**	.046***
	(3.12)	(4.26)
Constant	.539***	.138+
	(6.41)	(1.66)
Number of observations	431	429
Standard error of regression	.143	.125
R^2 (%)	78	90

NOTE: Numbers in parentheses are *t*-statistics (coefficients/standard errors).
$^+p \leq .1$.
$^*p \leq .05$.
$^{**}p \leq .01$.
$^{***}p \leq .001$.

liberal initiatives on women's issues, they are defecting from their party's standard conservative position toward these issues.

The difficulty of opposing one's own party is illustrated by the decline in Republican women's support for women's issues once their party gained the majority. With the privileges of majority membership

Table 20   The 103rd and 104th Congresses: OLS Regression Models on Reproductive Issue Roll-Call Votes

	Reproductive Issue	
Independent Variables	103rd Congress	104th Congress
Republican women	.42***	.506***
	(4.79)	(4.95)
Democratic women	.027	.081*
	(1.05)	(2.39)
Republican men	.079	.29***
	(1.12)	(3.25)
Ideology	−.8***	−.831***
	(−10.72)	(−10.06)
African-American representative	.016	−.112
	(.22)	(−1.11)
Religion	−.09***	−.113***
	(−3.36)	(−3.86)
Freshman	.049+	−.019
	(1.95)	(−.64)
% Vote for Clinton	.045	.321
	(.23)	(1.32)
% Vote for Perot	.507*	.552
	(2.1)	(1.56)
Southern	−.028	.062+
	(−.93)	(1.76)
% Black	.01	.203
	(.06)	(1.04)
% Urban	.049	−.003
	(.71)	(−.03)
Median household income	.065***	.101***
	(3.85)	(4.94)
Constant	.12	−.144
	(1.01)	(−.84)
Number of observations	431	429
Standard error of regression	.223	.249
R^2 (%)	71	70

NOTE: Numbers in parentheses are *t*-statistics (coefficients/standard errors).
+$p \leq .1$.
*$p \leq .05$.
**$p \leq .01$.
***$p \leq .001$.

comes the added pressure to maintain unity in order to keep control of the policy agenda and the procedural advantages associated with majority status. The pressure for party loyalty was especially acute in the 104th Congress, when the Republican leadership worked to demonstrate party unity by passing the ten elements of the Contract with

America, including the welfare reform bill, in the first hundred days of the congressional session. Therefore, while the coefficient for Republican women remained a significant predictor of liberal women's issue voting in the 104th Congress, being a Republican woman only increased the probability of voting for these issues by 13 percent.

Under the more conservative leadership of the 104th Congress, being a Democratic woman exerted a small (approximately 4 percent) but significant influence on women's issue voting. The increased importance of Democratic women reflects the new party dynamics. Majority party leaders work to solidify their party's control over the agenda by structuring choices on the House floor to reflect the preferences of their party members and to lure away votes from the minority party (Cox and McCubbins 1993). Thus, in the 104th Congress, the Republicans successfully attracted the support of some conservative male Democrats, while during the 103rd Congress, the Democrats were able to lure the votes of moderate Republicans. However, in the 104th Congress, traditional district characteristics greatly outweighed the importance of gender as a predictor of women's issue voting, particularly the level of Democratic support in the district as measured by the 1992 vote for President Clinton and the level of independence in the district represented by the 1992 vote for Ross Perot. The fact that the traditional determinants of congressional roll-call voting, such as ideology, party affiliation, and constituency characteristics, were all more important guides to a legislator's voting behavior than was gender in the 104th Congress indicates that in this more ideologically charged legislative session, all members stayed close to party lines.

The analysis of the subset of reproductive issues in table 20 indicates that the importance of gender is largely due to congresswomen's support for these feminist votes, which have direct consequences for women as a societal group. Across both Congresses, Republican women maintained a liberal voting record on reproductive issues. In the 103rd Congress, the presence of a moderate Republican woman increased the likelihood that a member would cast a liberal vote on reproductive issues by 42 percent. While both moderate Republican men and women serving in the 104th Congress were more likely to cast pro-choice votes than their conservative Republican colleagues were, moderate Republican women supported reproductive rights at almost twice the rate of moderate Republican men. Thus, the presence of a Republican woman increased the probability of voting liberally on reproductive issues by 51 percent while the presence of a moderate Republican man increased the probability of casting a liberal vote on reproductive rights by only 29 percent. In

fact, in the 104th Congress, only ideology was a more important predictor of liberal voting on reproductive issues than was the presence of a
moderate Republican woman. As with the full set of women's issues, being a Democratic woman also became a small but significant predictor
of voting on reproductive issues in the 104th Congress as Republicans
successfully attracted the votes of conservative male Democrats.

Reproductive Issues: Exposing Internal Party Tensions

The stability of Republican women's voting patterns on reproductive
issues across the two Congresses lends support to the assertion that
social issues like abortion are part of a set of cultural and civil rights
issues that have the potential to disrupt the traditional economic and
class-based cleavages that have divided the Republican and Democratic
parties since the New Deal (Carmines and Stimson 1989; Wolbrecht
2000; Sanbonmatsu 2002). As a group, the votes constituting the reproductive issues drew the most defections within each party. For example,
in the 103rd Congress, thirty-nine Republicans defected from their party
to support the Freedom of Access to (Abortion) Clinic Entrances Act,
while forty-three Democrats opposed the bill. Similarly, in the 104th
Congress, forty-five Republicans opposed the Smith Amendment restricting funding for international family planning programs, while
thirty-six Democrats defected from their party to support this pro-life
amendment.

The most fervent pro-choice and pro-life members have formed al-
liances with the relevant interest groups and created their own internal
member caucuses outside of the party structure to generate new policy
proposals and plan strategies for achieving their goals.[7] In fact, over time
the Pro-Choice and Pro-Life Caucuses have developed their own whip
structures outside of the party leadership to marshal votes when reproductive issues come to the floor. On those occasions when one group
finds a proposal that will split the support of the opposing side, the losing party leadership will not even engage the party's whip organization
and will refer to the vote as a "vote of conscience." For example, the
Partial Birth Abortion Act, which was vetoed by Democratic President
Bill Clinton, passed the House in the 104th Congress with seventy-two
Democratic votes, almost 40 percent of the Democratic Caucus, including the votes of the minority leader, Richard Gephardt (D-MO) and
the minority whip, David Bonior (D-MI). When interviewed, the bill's
sponsor, a conservative Republican congressman, explained that he first
offered the bill in the 103rd Congress, as a committee amendment to

the Freedom of Choice Act (before the procedure was called partial birth abortion). He saw that it "threw the pro-choice people off and caused consternation within their ranks. The issue resonates and it had the Democrats sweating." When he became Constitution Subcommittee chair in the 104th Congress, he decided to offer it as a freestanding bill.[8]

While Republican and Democratic women maintained a commitment to pro-choice voting across the two Congresses, logit analyses of individual votes on nonreproductive issues (models not shown) reflect more traditional partisan and constituency-focused voting patterns. For example, in the 104th Congress, Republicans who voted to raise the minimum wage held more liberal ideological views and represented lower-income districts that were more likely to support the Democratic candidate, Bill Clinton, for president in 1992. Even on some feminist issues, such as the Family and Medical Leave Act in the 103rd Congress and the two votes dealing with homosexual rights in the 104th Congress, Democratic and Republican women were not significantly more likely to cast liberal votes on these issues than were their male colleagues.

The vote on the Family and Medical Leave Act demonstrates the difference in the level of commitment needed to bring an issue onto the national agenda versus simply expressing a preference on the vote for final passage. By the time the Family and Medical Leave Act became law in 1993, the Bush administration had vetoed it twice. When Pat Schroeder (D-CO) offered one of the first family and medical leave bills in 1985, House members did not take the bill seriously. Both the Reagan Administration and the powerful Chamber of Commerce strongly opposed the idea, and Schroeder could not get any cosponsors for almost six months. Over the eight years from the introduction of the first leave bills to final passage in 1993, congresswomen, particularly Schroeder on the Democratic side and Marge Roukema (R-NJ) on the Republican side, played key roles in gaining publicity for the issue, lobbying committee leaders to take up the bill, and negotiating compromises on the legislative language (Foerstel and Foerstel 1996; Bingham 1997). Thus, the largely partisan vote on the Family and Medical Leave Act masks the pivotal role that women played in educating their colleagues and the public about the issue and brokering the deals that provided the substance of the bill and allowed it to come to the floor for a vote.

Conclusion

The analysis of women's issue roll-call voting indicates that although ideology is the main force guiding legislators' voting decisions, gender does play a significant role in determining how legislators vote on women's issues. The importance of gender stems largely from the voting behavior of Republican women. While both Democratic men and women are likely to cast liberal votes on women's issues, Republican women must defect from their party's traditional conservative stand on these issues. The dramatic decline in Republican women's support for liberal positions on women's issues in the 104th Congress highlights the tremendous risks inherent in and the difficulty of opposing one's party on the House floor, particularly as a member of the majority party.

As the majority party, Republicans also used their control over the congressional agenda to structure choices in a way that would create splits within the minority party. While Democratic women remained committed to liberal positions on women's issues, Republicans successfully attracted the votes of conservative Democratic men, particularly on the abortion issue.

Finally, the analysis of the subset of reproductive issues demonstrates that gender is one of the most important predictors of pro-choice voting on issues including family planning, federal funding of abortion, and sex education. In contrast to the broader set of women's issues, the voting patterns of Republican women on reproductive issues remained stable across the two Congresses. The tremendous increase in the number of votes taken on reproductive issues since Republicans gained the majority in the 104th Congress highlights the intensity of Republican women's commitment to pro-choice causes, as these women had to speak out constantly against a majority of their own party.

Chapter 8

Conclusion: Does Electing Women Matter?
The Impact on Policy Development and Democracy

Before women even gained the right to vote, Progressive Era women's groups lobbied their state and national government leaders to appoint women to school boards, public health agencies, and other community service entities (Skocpol 1992). Today, the approach of each election year finds women's groups, particularly feminist groups, donating money to women candidates, organizing candidate-training seminars for women, and actively campaigning for women candidates. When Americans go to the polls to cast their votes for a new representative, does it matter if the party nominee is a woman?

In addition to arguments based on equality, the close examination of members' legislative activity in the 103rd and 104th Congresses demonstrates that the personal identity of our representatives does have tangible policy consequences. These policy consequences affect our understanding of representational democracy, the congressional policy-making process, and relations between the political parties.

Issues of Representation: The Importance of Diversity

While the imperatives of reelection every two years dictate that legislators will pay close attention to the needs of their districts, the demands of the district constituencies are best viewed as guidelines for members' legislative activity rather than specific policy directives. Within the boundaries of constituency preferences, representatives are free to develop specific legislative priorities. In addition to pursuing programs for their districts and tending to committee responsibilities, personal interests based on politically significant social identities such as race and gender, occupational background, and individual experience will determine whether legislators focus their resources on breast cancer research or Parkinson's disease, violence against women or minimum mandatory sentences for drug offenders, a child-care tax credit or lowering capital gains tax rates. Thus, increasing membership diversity within the legislature will expand the range of issues and interests addressed by the congressional agenda.

The impact of social identities such as gender cannot be captured by a simple review of representatives' roll-call votes. Although two liberal Democrats may both take a feminist position on a roll-call vote concerning abortion, family and medical leave, or welfare reform, to understand fully how interests become incorporated into law, one must examine the entire policy-making process. The careful analysis of legislative activity at five different stages of the policy process demonstrates that Democratic and moderate Republican congresswomen are more committed to the pursuit of women's interests than are their male partisan colleagues. They have focused attention on new issues, particularly feminist issues, and have helped define formerly private concerns such as child care and domestic violence as public policy problems. The fact that gender differences are greatest in the area of bill sponsorship demonstrates that when representatives are the least constrained by seniority, committee position, and the demands of party loyalty, they can most clearly express their unique policy priorities. Therefore, given the opportunity, female representatives will work to incorporate the interests of women, children, and families into the congressional agenda.

At this point, the small number of conservative women in Congress makes it difficult to determine whether conservative women will ignore women's issues altogether or pursue these issues as priorities from an antifeminist point of view. The evidence from the 104th Congress indicates that it was conservative Republican men who took the lead in drafting antifeminist proposals and shepherding them through the legislative process. The conservative women generally pursued other policy interests. When they did engage in antifeminist causes, however, they adopted a supporting role, lending their names as cosponsors or speaking on the floor, particularly on abortion, at the request of bill sponsors.

A member's level of commitment to women's issues is particularly important in the current era of budget politics in which Republicans and Democrats are competing to define themselves as the more fiscally responsible party. As individual programs compete for funding, one representative's wasteful pork barrel project is another's essential program. Politically significant social identities such as gender and race will play a more central role in the decision calculus of legislators when the results of the bill will have direct consequences for the representative's social group. As one Democratic congresswoman explained it, women are more active on issues like family planning, sexual harassment, and child-support enforcement because "women have the most at risk." Thus, during the 106th Congress, it was the Democratic women on the Education and Workforce Committee who drafted the amendment and led the fight to reinstate gender equity provisions into the Republican bill to reauthorize the programs under the Elementary and Secondary Education Act. In negotiations on the same bill, it was the Hispanic Democrats who were willing to fall on their swords to save bilingual education programs, even when the Democratic presidential administration expressed a willingness to compromise on those programs.[1] Therefore, it is critical for women and minorities to have a seat at the table when legislators negotiate the final deals on public policy.

The Congressional Policy-Making Process: The Influence of the Institutional and Political Contexts

Regardless of their abstract policy preferences, I have shown that the choices legislators make concerning which policies to pursue depends on the limitations of their positions within the institution and their assessment of the political context. For example, the analysis of the bill sponsorship patterns of representatives demonstrates that Democratic and Republican women initiated more social welfare proposals than did their male partisan colleagues only when they had access to the prerogatives of the majority party. Since the majority party controls the overall content and direction of the policy agenda and social welfare issues make up a large portion of the legislation considered by the committees, congresswomen of both parties determined that the increased opportunity to influence policy on these issues justified the expense of political capital on developing and advocating social welfare policies.

While representatives campaign on promises to initiate legislation to provide prescription drug coverage for seniors and to reform the educational system, they have the most influence over policies within the jurisdiction of their committees. The fact that the majority of congresswomen were elected in the 1992 Year-of-the-Woman elections or later limits their influence on policy because they lack the seniority to gain appointments to prestige committees such as Ways and Means, which has jurisdiction over issues including welfare reform and Medicare. Similarly, few women command the seniority necessary to advance to leadership positions on the committees and subcommittees. Since the committee and subcommittee chairs draft the legislative vehicles that are subject to committee markups and their bills are the most likely to gain floor consideration and become law, congresswomen who want to influence policy on women's issues must convince the committee leaders to accept their proposals.

The examination of amending behavior in committees indicates that expanding the seats at the committee table to include more women will have an impact on the nature of the problems considered by the committees and expand the realm of legitimate solutions to a problem. In the 103rd Congress, Democratic women utilized their committee positions to encourage their Democratic colleagues to incorporate more gender-related proposals into committee legislation, while in the 104th Congress these women used their committee seats as a platform to vehemently oppose conservative Republican initiatives on women's issues. Similarly, in the 104th Congress, moderate Republican women sought to moderate their party's proposals on such issues as welfare reform by offering amendments to expand child-support enforcement and women's access to child care. Moreover, legislators and staff maintain that congresswomen bring a different perspective to committee deliberations on all issues. Clearly, a seat on a powerful committee provides a member of a politically significant minority group with the tools to fight for inclusion of his or her group's interests into the ultimate policy solution.

The Politics of Defection

Interest group advocates and media commentators often express disappointment that a legislator did not take a stand for principle on a particular issue or vote in the way one would expect them to vote as a representative of a particular social group. My research demonstrates that, beyond the views of the district constituency, representatives carefully assess the nature of the political context before they decide to pursue priorities that are not in line with the views of the majority of their party caucus and important party interest group supporters.

Women's issues constitute an area where the preferences of moderate Republicans, particularly women, often diverge from their more conservative party colleagues. The analysis of the legislative behavior of moderate Republicans in the 103rd and 104th Congresses indicates that these representatives found it easier to pursue liberal stands on women's issues as members of the minority party. As minority party legislators, moderate Republicans were simply expected to bring along their contingent of votes; however, when they ascended to the majority they had to oppose their party colleagues more aggressively in order to incorporate their policy views into legislation or eliminate offending provisions. In addition, moderate Republicans had to take this more aggressive stance when their party commanded the stronger sanctions that come with majority power. Majority status yields opportunities for a representative to achieve action on their policy priorities on a wide range of issues. However, moderate Republicans who antagonized party colleagues and important party supporters such as social conservatives risked the retaliation of party and committee leaders. For example, leaders might refuse to incorporate funding for a cherished district project into the appropriations bills or they might exclude a representative's proposals on other issues from committee legislation. The costs of defection are exacerbated when a president of the same party occupies the White House. For example, moderate Republicans in the current Congress face additional pressure to support their party leader, President Bush.

The evidence from the interviews and regression analyses shows that, as majority party members, moderate Republicans pursued their more liberal views on women's issues with a close eye on what party colleagues would bear. The analysis of the bill sponsorship patterns of legislators indicates that when moderate Republican women ascended to the majority in the 104th Congress, they shifted their resources from developing feminist proposals, which Republicans generally oppose, to a greater focus on social welfare initiatives. Furthermore, these women drastically reduced their support for liberal positions on women's issue roll-call votes and thus stayed closer to party lines.

At the same time that the pressure to support the party becomes more intense, members of a potentially strategic voting block will become the focus of more aggressive lobbying efforts from opposition interest groups. Thus, moderate Republicans, especially women, received more attention from liberal interest groups who viewed them as the last hope to preserve social welfare programs or eliminate conservative initiatives on reproductive rights. These moderates had to negotiate the competing pressures of working to achieve their policy goals on women's issues without damaging their credibility within the Republican conference by being perceived as advocates for Democratic interest groups. Therefore, as often as possible, moderates pursued their policy goals within the boundaries of what their natural allies, fellow Republicans, could accept and they lobbied their party colleagues to expand those boundaries by incorporating more gender-related concerns into party legislation.

Thus, the politics of defection is a complicated balancing act, the dynamics of which have far-reaching implications for our understanding of congressional policy making. This effort to balance contradictory policy preferences with party loyalty likely extends beyond moderate Republican women who support liberal positions on women's issues to pro-environment Republicans, fiscally conservative Democrats, and other legislators who espouse policy positions that contravene the prevailing view within their party caucus.

Women and Party Competition: Strategic Uses of the Electoral Connection

When scholars point to the power of the electoral connection, they generally refer to the fact that legislators concerned about reelection will closely follow the wishes of their individual district constituencies. My research shows that legislators who represent strategically important groups can also utilize electoral concerns as a tool to advance the policy interests of their group and as a means to acquire power within their party conferences. In the current era of close party competition, in which a court battle determined the 2000 presidential race and Republicans saw their level of control reduced to a razor-thin margin in the House of Representatives and an evenly split Senate later turned over to the Democrats by the defection of one Republican Senator, both parties are actively courting the support of groups they believe could be swayed to their corner with the right message. The expansion of the gender gap since the 1980s has encouraged both parties to compete actively for the women's vote. Both Republican and Democratic congresswomen use their connection to women as a politically significant social group as leverage to advance their policy goals on women's issues and to gain power within their party conferences.

For the political parties, the crafting of the strategy to sell a policy to the public is as important as the content. Thus, both Democratic and Republican leaders are looking for policies to attract women voters, and they turn to congresswomen to help promote those policies. This concern with the gender gap provides Democratic and Republican women with an opportunity to advance policies related to women's interests, raise their public profiles, and attain power within their party caucuses. Interest groups and individual legislators from both parties seek out women to sponsor or cosponsor gender-related legislation not simply because they have expertise in a particular area but also because they want to connect themselves to the symbolic moral authority these women have as women and/or as mothers.

On the House floor and in press conferences, party leaders rely on women as spokespersons and political symbols in their effort to demonstrate that their party is protecting women's interests. Thus, Democratic leaders turn to their congresswomen to expand the party's traditional advantage with female voters by promoting Democratic initiatives on women's issues and branding Republican policies as antifamily and antiwomen. Similarly, Republicans utilize Republican women to combat Democratic efforts to paint their proposals as hurting women. Republican women also craft messages to explain how traditional Republican issues, such as tax cuts, will benefit women. By speaking out on behalf of their party, female legislators raise their own public profile and collect favors that they can use to advance their positions within the party conference, attain support for favored policy initiatives, or gain leeway to defect from their party's position on another issue.

The politics of the gender gap demonstrate that when a majority group perceives a minority interest as strategically important to the advancement of the majority's electoral fortunes, then minority members can leverage that concern to gain influence within the institution beyond their numbers. Thus, as with the gender gap, the more recent emergence of Hispanics as a subject of electoral competition between the parties has raised the profile of Hispanic representatives within their parties. While partisan concern over the gender gap has helped individual congresswomen in their efforts to advance specific policy proposals or their own position within the institution, this road to power cannot match the influence conferred by appointment to a prestigious committee or advancement to a committee leadership position. Moreover, the power derived from electoral sources such as the gender gap is highly contingent on the centrality of the group and its interests to the party's voting coalition. As concerns about defense and ways to combat terrorism dominate the Congressional agenda, the ability of women to capitalize on issues related to the gender gap is diminished.

Conclusion

By carefully examining the legislative priorities of members across all stages of the policy process, this research demonstrates that in addition to advocating for the needs of their districts, female legislators do exhibit a profound commitment to the pursuit of policies for women, children, and families. Both Democratic and moderate Republican women used their bill sponsorship and cosponsorship activity to focus attention on women's issues, and they championed gender-related proposals in their committee and floor activity. Congresswomen's consistent advocacy of women's issue initiatives, particularly feminist initiatives, demonstrates an intensity of commitment that could not be captured merely by a study of roll-call votes. Their unique policy priorities indicate that increasing the presence of women in Congress could open the congressional agenda to more gender-related concerns. Additionally, the important relationship between social identity and the intensity of commitment to issues that have a direct impact on their social group holds significant implications for understanding the influence of other politically significant social identities, including race and sexual orientation, on the policy priorities of individual legislators.

However, simply increasing the number of women and other minorities in Congress will not automatically lead to enhanced influence on policy design, since presence in the institution does not directly translate into power over legislative outcomes. While it is significant that increasing numbers of women are elected to Congress, my research demonstrates that the ability of congresswomen to legislate on behalf of women is constrained by their position within the institution, particularly their level of seniority, access to committee positions, and status as a member of the majority/minority party.

The fact that most of the women serving in Congress were elected in the 1992 Year-of-the-Woman elections and in more recent elections means that women as a group lack seniority. Therefore, their access to leadership positions within the committees and their party caucuses has been extremely limited, thus denying women the significant power over the shaping of public policy that comes with such positions. Similarly, until women gain more seats on prestigious committees with broad legislative jurisdictions such as Ways and Means, Appropriations, and Energy and Commerce, their ability to bring their gender-related concerns and their unique experience to the policy-making table is diminished. Furthermore, status as a member of the majority or minority party regulates the extent of a legislator's influence. Both Republican and Democratic women were more aggressive and effective advocates for women's issues as members of the majority party because majority status brings agenda control and an opportunity to achieve action on one's most cherished legislative priorities. The fact that most women in Congress are Democrats means that women are currently concentrated in the minority party, a position that greatly inhibits their ability to influence the direction of policy on women's issues.

Finally, the political context—including the configuration of interest groups, the intensity of opinion within the party caucuses, the level of competition between the parties, and the priorities of the president— has an impact on the decision calculus of representatives concerning which policies to pursue. Political context effects are magnified when representatives are pursuing initiatives that contravene the majority view of their party caucus. Thus, when moderate Republican women seek to address gender-related concerns, they must work within the parameters of what their party colleagues will accept; otherwise they risk being perceived as advocates for opposition party interest groups. In negotiations over the details of a policy, these women do use their political capital to try to expand the boundaries of what their partisan counterparts will accept. However, if they antagonize party colleagues, these natural allies may not support their initiatives in other areas. Therefore, my findings concerning the influence of women suggest that moderate Republicans, socially conservative Democrats, and defense-hawk Democrats must maintain a careful balancing act between preferences and power considerations, since they are potentially pivotal voters for policies generally favored by the opposition party.

The competing pressures to pursue their policy goals and to conform to the established party position are exacerbated when a representative is in the majority party and viewed as the last bulwark against disaster by opposition interest groups. Similarly, the election of a president of their own party increases the costs of defection. Therefore, moderate Republican women who advocate gender-related concerns in the current Congress will face even more pressure to conform than those who served in the 104th Congress under a Democratic president, as they will not only be contradicting their party leaders but their president as well.

In the final analysis, understanding how politically significant social identities have an impact on the legislative behavior of representatives is not simply a matter of raw numbers in the legislature. The interplay of presence and power is complex. In the case of gender, the unique policy interests of women provide substantive support to those who call for the inclusion of more women in the cabinet choices of presidents and governors and the leadership ranks of Congress and the state legislatures. Electing women has important consequences for the quality of our representational system, thus making the call for more diversity in Congress more than a mere platitude. Presence, however, is only a first step. Power in Congress also depends on access to influential positions within the institution that allow members to exercise strategic influence over the shape of policy outcomes.

Identifying Committees and Subcommittees
That Considered Women's Issue Bills

A member's committee assignment is a key determinant of the range of policies he or she will be able to influence during his or her congressional career. Given the important institutional advantages of agenda control and staff expertise held by committee and subcommittee members, it is essential to include measures of institutional position in the models of legislative activity. Unfortunately, women's issues do not fall within clear committee jurisdictions. Therefore, the committee and subcommittee variables are designed to capture which legislators had the greatest opportunity to influence policy on women's issues.

To create the first set of committee and subcommittee variables, which I employed in the models for bill sponsorship and cosponsorship, I developed a coding scheme that first takes into account the number of bills a committee or subcommittee considered through either hearings or a legislative markup. Since most bills never see committee action, I also tracked how many women's issue bills were referred to but never considered by each committee. In his study of the evolution of committee jurisdictions, King (1997) found that bill referral is an even more important determinant of committee jurisdiction than the statutory rules of jurisdiction because committees try to gain control over ambiguous policy areas by developing a record of bill referrals on the issue. Hardin (1998) also examines bill referral in his study of the evolution of congressional committee jurisdictions on health issues from 1979 to 1993.

Using the joint criteria of committee action and bill referral, I created variables for "seat on a woman's issue committee" and "seat on a woman's issue subcommittee." I used the same methods to characterize subcommittees as feminist and social welfare. Thus, these institutional variables capture the committees and subcommittees that considered the most women's issues legislation. Therefore, they do not represent the only committees or subcommittees that considered women's issue bills. Instead they represent an effort to isolate committee members that should have the most potential expertise in and jurisdiction over women's issues.

In addition to these subcommittee variables, I also created measures of committee and subcommittee leadership by including variables for woman's committee chairs and ranking minority members as well as subcommittee chairs and ranking members. Among committee members, the committee and subcommittee chairs are the most powerful legislators. They control the committee staff and exercise agenda control by deciding which bills to bring up for a markup and by guiding the debate. On the minority side, the ranking minority members are the most powerful legislators in the committee's minority contingent. These members control the minority staff, and they are the first legislators the chairs will turn to when they are trying to broker a compromise with the minority.

Since the analysis of committee amendments only includes those bills that advanced to a committee markup, the subcommittee variables used in the committee amending behavior models account for the legislators with seats on the subcommittees that considered the most women's issue bills and amendments. These variables were created by measuring the number of women's issue bills considered by each committee and subcommittee as well as the number of amendments offered to each of these bills. I also took into account which subcommittees held hearings or markups on the bills. Similarly, the floor amendment models only include amendments offered to those bills that were debated on the House floor. Therefore, the committee variables used in these models account for the number of committee and subcommittee bills that reached the House floor and the number of amendments offered to these bills.

The committee and subcommittee variables used throughout the study are listed below. The number two in parentheses indicates that the members of this committee or subcommittee considered the greatest number of women's issue proposals during that Congressional session; therefore, members of that committee or subcommittee were assigned a value of 2 on a 0, 1, 2 scale. The committee and subcommittee chair and ranking member variables correspond to the chair and ranking members of the listed committees and subcommittees.

COMMITTEE VARIABLES

103rd and 104th Congresses: Seat on a Committee That Considered Women's Issue Legislation[1]—

Education and Labor [104th Economic and Educational Opportunities] (2), Energy and Commerce [104th Commerce], Judiciary, and Ways and Means.

This variable was generally dropped in favor of the more discriminating subcommittee variables. However, the Woman's Committee Chair and Ranking Member variables used throughout the study reflect the chairs and ranking members of these committees.

SUBCOMMITTEE VARIABLES EMPLOYED IN THE BILL SPONSORSHIP AND COSPONSORSHIP ANALYSES

103rd Congress: Seat on a Subcommittee That Considered Women's Issue Legislation—

Appropriations: Labor, Health and Human Services, and Education
Education and Labor: Elementary, Secondary, and Vocational Education; Select Education and Civil Rights
Energy and Commerce: Health and Environment

Judiciary: Crime and Criminal Justice; Civil and Constitutional Rights
Post Office and Civil Service: Compensation and Employee Benefits

104th Congress: Seat on a Subcommittee That Considered Women's Issue Legislation—

Appropriations: Labor, Health and Human Services, and Education
Economic and Educational Opportunities: Early Childhood, Youth and Families; Post-Secondary Education, Training and Life Long Learning; Employer-Employee Relations; Workforce Protections
Commerce: Health and Environment
Judiciary: Crime
Ways and Means: Health

103rd Congress: Seat on a Subcommittee That Considered Feminist Legislation—

Appropriations: Labor, Health and Human Services, and Education
Education and Labor: Labor-Management Relations; Select Education and Civil Rights
Energy and Commerce: Health and Environment
Judiciary: Crime and Criminal Justice; Civil and Constitutional Rights
Post Office and Civil Service: Compensation and Employee Benefits

104th Congress: Seat on a Subcommittee That Considered Feminist Legislation—

Appropriations: Labor, Health and Human Services, and Education
Economic and Educational Opportunities: Workforce Protections
Commerce: Health and Environment
Judiciary: Crime; Constitution
Ways and Means: Human Resources

103rd Congress: Seat on a Subcommittee That Considered Social Welfare Legislation—

Appropriations: Labor, Health and Human Services, and Education
Education and Labor: Elementary, Secondary, and Vocational Education
Energy and Commerce: Health and Environment
Judiciary: Crime and Criminal Justice
Ways and Means: Health

104th Congress: Seat on a Subcommittee That Considered Social Welfare Legislation—

Appropriations: Labor, Health and Human Services, and Education
Economic and Educational Opportunities: Early Childhood, Youth and Families; Post-Secondary Education, Training and Life Long Learning; Employer-Employee Relations

Commerce: Health and Environment
Judiciary: Crime
Ways and Means: Health

SUBCOMMITTEE VARIABLES EMPLOYED IN THE ANALYSIS OF COMMITTEE
AMENDING BEHAVIOR

103rd Congress: Seat on a Subcommittee That Considered Women's Issue Amendments—

This variable is used in the analysis of the full set of women's issue amendments and the subset of social welfare amendments.

Appropriations: Labor, Health and Human Services, and Education
Education and Labor: Elementary, Secondary, and Vocational Education (2);
Labor-Management Relations
Energy and Commerce: Health and Environment
Judiciary: Crime and Criminal Justice
Ways and Means: Health

103rd Congress: Seat on a Subcommittee that Considered Feminist Amendments—

Appropriations: Labor, Health and Human Services, and Education
Education and Labor: Labor-Management Relations; Select Education and Civil
Rights
Energy and Commerce: Health and Environment
Judiciary: Crime and Criminal Justice; Civil and Constitutional Rights
Post Office and Civil Service: Compensation and Employee Benefits

104th Congress: Seat on a Subcommittee That Considered Women's Issue Amendments—

This variable is used in the analysis of the full set of women's issue amendments and the subset of social welfare amendments.

Appropriations: Labor, Health and Human Services, and Education
Economic and Educational Opportunities: Early Childhood, Youth and Families; Post-Secondary Education, Training and Life Long Learning; Employer-Employee Relations
Commerce: Health and Environment
Judiciary: Constitution; Immigration and Claims
Ways and Means: Health; Human Resources

104th Congress: Seat on a Subcommittee That Considered Feminist Amendments—

Appropriations: Labor, Health and Human Services, and Education
Economic and Educational Opportunities: Workforce Protections; Employer-Employee Relations

Commerce: Health and Environment
Judiciary: Crime; Constitution
Ways and Means: Human Resources

SUBCOMMITTEE VARIABLES EMPLOYED IN THE ANALYSIS OF FLOOR AMENDING BEHAVIOR

103rd Congress: Seat on a Subcommittee that Considered Women's Issue Amendments—

Appropriations: Labor, Health and Human Services, and Education
Education and Labor: Elementary, Secondary, and Vocational Education (2); Human Resources; Select Education and Civil Rights
Energy and Commerce: Health and Environment
Judiciary: Crime and Criminal Justice

104th Congress: Seat on a Subcommittee that Considered Women's Issue Amendments—

Appropriations: Labor, Health and Human Services, and Education
Economic and Educational Opportunities: Early Childhood, Youth and Families
Commerce: Health and Environment
Banking and Financial Services: Housing and Community Opportunity
Judiciary: Constitution; Crime
Ways and Means: Health; Human Resources

Appendix B

Women's Issue Bills Considered
in Committee Markup and/or on the Floor

Tables B1 and B2 below provide a detailed listing of the women's issue bills that advanced to a committee markup and/or floor debate. Each table includes the bill number and name, the subcommittees that held hearings or a markup on the bill, the committees that conducted a markup on the bill, the number of amendments offered to the bill in committee, the rule adopted for floor debate on the bill, and the number of amendments offered to the bill on the floor. An asterisk (∗) next to the number of amendments denotes bills that include only those amendments that were relevant to women's issues. For example, in the 103rd Congress, women's groups identified the Democrats' crime bill as an important piece of legislation for women because it included the Violence against Women Act and protections for children who are victims of abuse. Therefore, only amendments concerning crimes against women, children, and the elderly were included in the sample; all other amendments were excluded.

Fifty-eight bills in the 103rd Congress and sixty-three bills in the 104th Congress advanced to a committee markup. Among those bills considered in committee, thirty-seven of the fifty-eight bills in the 103rd Congress and forty-nine of the sixty-three bills in the 104th Congress were amended during the markup. The number of amendments offered to each bill ranges from a single amendment to a high of 219 amendments in eight committees for President Clinton's health care reform bill during the 103rd Congress, and ninety-six amendments in five committees for the final Republican welfare reform bill during the 104th Congress. In the 103rd Congress, 126 members offered 447 women's issue amendments. In the 104th Congress, 171 members sponsored 588 women's issue amendments.

At the floor level fifty-one of the bills considered in the 103rd Congress and sixty-one of the bills debated in the 104th Congress attracted women's issue amendments. The rules governing debate on these bills range from open rules, in which any member can offer an amendment, to closed rules that exclude all amendments or only permit amendments offered by the reporting committee. Within these two extremes, the rules governing debate can specify which sections of a bill can be amended, the number of amendments that can be offered, and, sometimes, which individual members can offer the amendments. Bills that pass under suspension of the rules motions are generally noncontroversial because they cannot be amended on the floor and require a two-thirds House majority to pass (Oleszek 1996).

The number of amendments offered to each bill ranges from zero to a high of fifty-one amendments to a bill reauthorizing the Elementary and Secondary Education Act (ESEA) in the 103rd Congress and thirty-one amendments to a low-income housing bill in the 104th Congress. During the 103rd Congress, 101 legislators offered 226 women's issue floor amendments. During the 104th Congress, 130 legislators sponsored 246 women's issue floor amendments.

Those legislators who offered amendments in committee and on the floor sponsored a mix of first-degree, second-degree, and procedural amendments. First-degree amendments include straight amendments, substitute amendments, and amendments to the substitute. Second-degree amendments are amendments to amendments and amendments to amendments to a substitute. Procedural amendments include, for example, points of order challenging the germaneness of an amendment, motions to table a bill and thus halt a committee markup, motions to recommit a bill to committee with or without instructions, motions to discharge a bill from committee, motions to go to conference, and motions to pass a conference report.

Table B1 The 103rd Congress: Amendments Offered to Women's Issue Bills in Committee Markup and/or on the Floor

HR Bill No.	Bill Name	Subcommittee Hearing or Markup	Committee Markup		Floor	
			Committee Name	No. of Amendments	Rule	No. of Amendments
6	Improving America's Schools Act of 1994	ESV, CSPP	Education and Labor	47	Open	51
1804	Goals 2000: Educate America Act	ESV	Education and Labor	20	Modified open	9
2884	School-to-Work Opportunities Act of 1993	N.A.	Education and Labor	8	Suspension of rules	3
3842	Head Start Act Amendments of 1994	N.A.	Education and Labor	5	N.A.	N.A.
4250	Head Start Act and Community Services Block Grant Act, Authorizations, FY 1994	N.A.	Education and Labor	0	Suspension of rules	1
2010	National Service Trust Act of 1993	SECR, HR	Education and Labor	13	Modified open	26
856	Educational Research, Development, and Dissemination Excellence Act	SECR	Education and Labor	1	Suspension of rules	1
8	Healthy Meals for Healthy Americans Act of 1994	ESV, DON	Education and Labor, Agriculture	8	Suspension of rules	1
1237	National Child Protection Act of 1993	CCR	Judiciary	0	Suspension of rules	1
3694	Child Abuse Accountability Act of 1993	CEB	Post Office and Civil Service	1	Suspension of rules	1
3993	Child Sexual Abuse Prevention Act of 1994	CCJ	Judiciary	0		
3378	International Parental Kidnapping Crime Act of 1993	N.A.	Judiciary	0	Suspension of rules	1
1308	Religious Freedom Restoration Act of 1993	CCR	Judiciary	0	Suspension of rules	2
4570	Child Support Responsibility Act of 1994	CEB, MFP	Post Office and Civil Service	2	N.A.	N.A.
965	Child Safety Protection Act	CCPC	Energy and Commerce	1	Suspension of rules	4

1120	Assaults against Children Act of 1994	CCJ	Judiciary	0	N.A.	N.A.
324	Jacob Wetterling Crimes against Children Registration Act	CCJ	Judiciary	0	Suspension of rules	1
5140	Child Support Obligations Enforcement Improvement Act	N.A.	N.A.	N.A.	Suspension of rules	1
454	Full Faith and Credit for Child Support Orders Act	ALGR	Judiciary	0	Suspension of rules	1
5179	Federal Employee Garnishment of Wages for Child Support Act of 1994	N.A.	N.A.	N.A.	Voice vote	1
4084	Community Services Block Grants Amendments of 1994	N.A.	Education and Labor	1	N.A.	N.A.
4085	Low-Income Home Energy Assistance Amendments of 1994	N.A.	Education and Labor	2	N.A.	N.A.
4034	Urban Recreation and At-Risk Youth Act of 1994	NP, OV	Natural Resources	1	Suspension of rules	1
796	Freedom of Access to Abortion Clinic Entrances Act of 1993	CCJ	Judiciary	4	Modified open	14
3313	Veterans Health Improvement Act of 1993	N.A.	Veterans' Affairs	4	Suspension of rules	4
2202	Public Health Service Act Amendment (Breast Cancer)	HE	Energy and Commerce	2	Suspension of rules	3
490	Conveyance of Lands to Columbia Hospital for Women	PBG	Public Works and Transportation	0	Suspension of rules	1
670	Family Planning Amendments Act of 1993	HE	Energy and Commerce	1	Modified open	9
2203	Public Health Service Act Amendment (STDs)	HE	Energy and Commerce	0	Suspension of rules	1
2201	Injury Prevention and Control Amendments of 1993	HE	Energy and Commerce	0	Suspension of rules	1
25	Freedom of Choice Act	CCR	Judiciary	9	N.A.	N.A.

(continued)

Table B1   (continued)

HR Bill No.	Bill Name	Subcommittee Hearing or Markup	Committee Markup			Floor	
			Commiette Name	No. of Amendments	Rule	Rule	No. of Amendments
4	National Institutes of Health Revitalization Act of 1993		Energy and Commerce	5	Modified open	Modified open	7
3869	Minority Health Improvement Act of 1994	HE	Energy and Commerce	10	Suspension of rules	Suspension of rules	1
2205	Trauma Care Systems Amendments of 1993	HE	Energy and Commerce	0	Suspension of rules	Suspension of rules	2
3600	Health Security Act (Clinton Health Reform Bill)	LMR, Health, HHC, MFP, HRIR	Education and Labor; Ways and Means; Natural Resources; Judiciary; Veterans' Affairs; Armed Forces; Government Operations; Post Office and Civil Service	219	N.A.	N.A.	N.A.
4801	Small Business Reauthorization and Amendment Act of 1994	N.A.	Small Business	0	Modified open	Modified open	1*
1632	District of Columbia Code, Title 11, Amendment	N.A.	District of Columbia	1	Suspension of rules	Suspension of rules	1
3013	Women's Bureau in Department of Veterans Affairs Act	N.A.	Veterans Affairs	0	Suspension of Rules	Suspension of Rules	1
4822	Congressional Accountability Act	N.A.	House Administration; Rules	16*	Modified open	Modified open	13
1032	Department of Veteran's Affairs Employment Discrimination Act	N.A.	Veteran's Affairs	4	Suspension of rules	Suspension of rules	1

2721	Federal Employee Fairness Act of 1993	SECR, CS	Education and Labor; Post Office and Civil Service	11	N.A.	N.A.
4263	Small Business and Minority Small Business Procurement Opportunities Act of 1994	N.A.	Small Business	10*	N.A.	N.A.
4297	Small Business Administration Amendments of 1994	N.A.	Small Business	3*	N.A.	N.A.
2238	Federal Acquisitions Improvement Act	N.A.	Government Operations	1*	N.A.	N.A.
1	Family and Medical Leave Act	LMR	Education and Labor; Post Office and Civil Service	14	Modified open	4
4361	Federal Employee Family Friendly Leave Act	CEB	Post Office and Civil Service	0	Suspension of rules	2
4278	Social Security Act Amendments of 1994 (Nanny Tax Bill)	N.A.	Ways and Means	0	Suspension of rules	2
3456	Surviving Spouses Benefits Act of 1993	N.A.	Veterans Affairs	1	Suspension of rules	1
2751	Federal Employees Humanitarian Leave Act of 1993	CEB	Post Office and Civil Service	0	Suspension of rules	1
3355	Violent Crime Control and Law Enforcement Act of 1994	N.A.	Judiciary	3*	Suspension of rules	9*
4092	Violent Crime Control and Law Enforcement Act of 1994	N.A.	N.A.	N.A.	Modified open	11*
1133	Violence against Women Act	CCJ	Judiciary	5	Suspension of rules	1
4031	Juvenile Prosecution Act of 1994	CCJ	Judiciary	2	N.A.	N.A.
3098	Youth Handgun Safety Act of 1993	CCJ	Judiciary	0	Suspension of rules	1
1152	Hate Crimes Sentencing Enhancement Act	CCJ	Judiciary	2	Suspension of rules	1

(continued)

HR Bill No.	Bill Name	Subcommittee Hearing or Markup	Committee Markup		Floor	
			Committee Name	No. of Amendments	Rule	No. of Amendments
1645	Poverty Data Improvement Act	N.A.	Post Office and Civil Service	0	Suspension of rules	1
5156	Technical Correction to the Food Stamp Act of 1977	N.A.	Agriculture	0	Voice Vote	1
3436	Food Stamp Act of 1977, Amendment	DON	Agriculture	0	Voice Vote	1
2518	Department of Labor, Health and Human Services, Education and Related Agencies Appropriations Act FY 94	LHHS	Appropriations	2*	Privileged	8*
4606	Department of Labor, Health and Human Services, Education and Related Agencies Appropriations Act FY 95	LHHS	Appropriations	6	Privileged	12*
4426	Foreign Operations FY 95	FO	Appropriations	N.A.	Modified open	1*
2492	District of Columbia FY 94	DC	Appropriations	N.A.	Privileged	1*
4649	District of Columbia FY 95	DC	Appropriations	N.A.	Privileged	2*
2403	Treasury, Postal Service and General Government FY 94	TPGG	Appropriations	N.A.	Open	1*
2264	Omnibus Budget Reconciliation Act of 1993	N.A.	Education and Labor; Agriculture	4*	N.A.	N.A.

NOTE: An asterisk (*) next to the number of amendments indicates bills that include only those amendments that were relevant to women's issues. N.A. = not applicable. The 103rd Congress subcommittees are as follows:

Agriculture:
Department Operations and Nutrition (DON)

Appropriations:
Labor, Health and Human Services, Education and Related Agencies (LHHS)
District of Columbia (DC)
Foreign Operations (FO)
Treasury, Postal Service, and General Government (TPSGG)
Armed Services:
Military Forces and Personnel (MFP)
Education and Labor:
Elementary, Secondary, and Vocational Education (ESV)
Human Resources (HR)
Labor-Management Relations (LMR)
Select Education and Civil Rights (SECR)
Energy and Commerce:
Commerce, Consumer Protection, and Competitiveness (CCPC)
Health and Environment (HE)
Government Operations:
Human Resources and Intergovernmental Relations (HRIR)
Judiciary:
Administrative Law and Government Relations (ALGR)
Civil and Constitutional Rights (CCR)
Crime and Criminal Justice (CCJ)
Natural Resources:
National Parks (NP)
Oversight (OV)
Post Office and Civil Service:
Census, Statistics, and Postal Personnel (CSPP)
Civil Service (CS)
Compensation and Employee Benefits (CEB)
Public Works and Transportation:
Public Buildings and Grounds (PBG)
Veterans' Affairs:
Hospitals and Health Care (HHC)
Ways and Means:
Health

Table B2   The 104th Congress: Amendments Offered to Women's Issue Bills in Committee Markup and/or on the Floor

HR Bill No.	Bill Name	Subcommittee Hearing or Markup	Committee Markup		Floor	
			Committee Name	No. of Amendments	Rule	No. of Amendments
2066	Healthy Meals for Children Act	N.A.	Economic and Educational Opportunities	1	Suspension of rules	1
1045	Goals 2000: Educate America Act, Amendment	N.A.	Economic and Educational Opportunities	0	Suspension of rules	1
3268	IDEA Improvement Act of 1996	ECYF	Economic and Educational Opportunities	14	Suspension of rules	1
4134	Immigration and Nationality Amendment Act (Deny public education to immigrants)	N.A.	N.A.	N.A.	Closed	0
1271	Family Privacy Protection Act of 1995	GMIT	Government Reform and Oversight	0	Open	2
1215	Contract with America Tax Relief Act of 1995	N.A.	Ways and Means	2	Modified closed	4
2288	Social Security Act Amendment	HR	Ways and Means	0	Voice vote	0
3286	Adoption Promotion and Stability Act of 1996	N.A.	Ways and Means Resources	5	Modified closed	1
1833	Partial Birth Abortion Ban Act of 1995	Const.	Judiciary	9	Closed	4
2425	Medicare Preservation Act of 1995	Health; HE	Ways and Means; Commerce	87	Modified closed	2
2976	Patient Right to Know Act of 1996	Health; HE	Commerce	0	N.A.	N.A.
3070	Health Coverage Availability and Affordability Act of 1996	HE	Commerce	12	N.A.	N.A.

3103	Health Insurance Portability and Accountability Act	N.A.	Ways and Means	13	Modified closed	5
995	ERISA Targeted Health Insurance Reform Act of 1995	EER	Economic and Educational Opportunities	3	N.A.	N.A.
831	Self-Employed Persons Health Care Deduction Extension Act of 1995	Health, OV	Ways and Means	10	Modified closed	3
1872	Ryan White CARE Act Amendments of 1995	HE	Commerce	0	Suspension of rules	1
3643	Veterans Benefits, Title 38, U.S.C, Amendment	HHC	Veterans Affairs	0	Suspension of rules	1
3118	Veterans' Health Care Eligibility Reform Act of 1996	HHC	Veterans Affairs	0	Suspension of rules	1
1627	Food Quality Protection Act of 1996	DONFA, HE	Agriculture; Commerce	2	Suspension of rules	1
2685	Medicare and Medicaid Coverage Data Bank Repeal	N.A.	Ways and Means	1	Voice vote	0
483	Medicare Select Policies Universal Expansion Act	Health, HE	Ways and Means; Commerce	4	Modified closed	3
1134	Medicare Presidential Budget Savings Extension Act	Health	Ways and Means	1	N.A.	N.A.
248	Public Health Service Act Amendment	HE	Commerce	1	Suspension of rules	1
3632	Social Security Act, Amendment	N.A.	Commerce	0	Suspension of rules	1
1747	Federally Supported Health Centers Act of 1995	N.A.	Commerce	1	Suspension of rules	1
3452	Presidential and Executive Office Accountability Act	GMIT	Government Reform and Oversight	3	Suspension of rules	2
3396	Defense of Marriage Act	Const.	Judiciary	6	Modified closed	5

(continued)

Table B2 (continued)

HR Bill No.	Bill Name	Subcommittee Hearing or Markup	Committee Markup		Floor	
			Committee Name	No. of Amendments	Rule	No. of Amendment
4036	Human Rights, Refugee, and Other Foreign Relations Provisions Act of 1996	N.A.	International Relations	0	Suspension of rules	2
956	Product Liability Fairness Act of 1995	N.A.	Judiciary	10*	Modified closed	9*
917	Common Sense Product Liability Reform Act	CTHM	Commerce	4	N.A.	N.A.
10	Common Sense Legal Reform Act of 1995	TF, CIP	Commerce	0	N.A.	N.A.
2391	Working Families Flexibility Act of 1996	WP	Economic and Educational Opportunities	1	Modified open	1
3448	Small Business Protection Act of 1996 (Minimum Wage/IRA for homemakers)	OV	Ways and Means	2*	Modified closed	1*
1227	Portal-to-Portal Act of 1947, Amendment	WP	Economic and Educational Opportunities	2	Modified closed	4
2531	Fair Labor Standards of 1938, Amendment	WP	Economic and Educational Opportunities	3	N.A.	N.A.
728	Local Government Law Enforcement Block Grants Act of 1995	N.A.	Judiciary	7*	Modified open	5*
665	Victims Justice Act of 1995	N.A.	Judiciary	0	Open	2
1533	Sexual Offender Tracking and Identification Act of 1996	Crime	Judiciary	0	Suspension of rules	1

1240	Sexual Crimes against Children Act of 1995	Crime	Judiciary	4	Suspension of rules	2
2137	Megan's Law	Crime	Judiciary	0	Suspension of rules	1
2974	Crimes against Children and Elderly Persons Increased Punishment Act	Crime	Judiciary	3	Open	8
2980	Interstate Stalking Punishment and Prevention Act	Crime	Judiciary	2	Suspension of rules	1
3456	Sexual Offender Tracking and Identification Act of 1996	N.A.	N.A.	N.A.	Suspension of rules	1
3676	Carjacking Correction Act of 1996	N.A.	Judiciary	0	Suspension of rules	1
4137	Drug Induced Rape Prevention and Punishment Act of 1996	N.A.	N.A.	N.A.	Suspension of rules	1
4	Personal Responsibility Act of 1995	HR, ECFY	Hearings Only—Ways and Means; Economic and Educational Opportunities	N.A.	Modified closed	28
1157	Welfare Transformation Act of 1995	HR	Ways and Means	71	N.A.	N.A.
3734	Personal Responsibility and Work Opportunity Act of 1996	HR	Ways and Means, Economic and Educational Opportunities; Agriculture; Commerce; Budget	96	Modified closed	5
1617	Consolidated and Reformed Education, Employment, and Rehabilitation Act (Job training programs)	ECYF, PETLL	Economic and Educational Opportunities	23	Open	9
1720	Government-Sponsored Enterprise Privatization Act of 1996 (Job training)	N.A.	Economic and Educational Opportunities	7	Suspension of rules	1

(continued)

Table B2 (continued)

HR Bill No.	Bill Name	Subcommittee Hearing or Markup	Committee Markup			Floor	
			Committee Name	No. of Amendments	Rule	No. of Amendments
2406	U.S. Housing Act of 1995	HCO	Banking and Financial Services	31	Open	31
2277	Legal Aid Act of 1995	CAL	Judiciary	21	N.A.	N.A.
999	Welfare Reform Consolidation Act of 1995	N.A.	Economic and Educational Opportunities	39	N.A.	N.A.
1135	Food Stamp Program and Commodity Distribution Act	N.A.	Agriculture	18	N.A.	N.A.
2202	Immigration Control and Financial Responsibility Act	IC	Judiciary	12*	Modified closed	4*
2703	Effective Death Penalty and Public Safety Act of 1996	N.A.	N.A.	N.A.	Modified Closed	1*
3735	Foreign Assistance Act of 1961, Amendment	N.A.	International Relations	1	N.A.	N.A.
2127	Department of Labor, Health and Human Services, Education and Related Agencies Appropriations Act FY 96	LHHS	Appropriations	32	Open	24*
3755	LHHS FY 97	LHHS	Appropriations	11	Open	25*
3450	Foreign Operations FY 97	FO	Appropriations	1*	Open	1*
1561	International Human Rights Act	H Rts.	International Relations	4*	Modified open	3*
1530	Defense Reauthorization 1995	MP	National Security	1*	Modified open	1*
3230	Defense Reauthorization 1996	MP	National Security	1*	Modified open	1*
2126	Department of Defense Appropriations Act FY 1996	NS	Appropriations	N.A.	Open	2*

Bill	Title	Subcommittee	Committee		Rule	Amendments
2076	Commerce, Justice, State FY 96	CJS	Appropriations	1*	Open	4*
3814	Commerce, Justice, State FY 96	CJS	Appropriations	N.A.	Open	6*
2546	District of Columbia FY 96	DC	Appropriations	3*	Modified open	4*
3845	District of Columbia FY 97	DC	Appropriations	2*	Open	1*
2020	Treasury, Postal Service, and General Government FY 96	TPSGG	Appropriations	1*	Open	1*
3756	Treasury, Postal Service, and General Government FY 97	TPSGG	Appropriations	2*	Open	2*
3019	Omnibus Consolidated Recissions and Appropriations Act of 1996	N.A.	Appropriations, Budget	N.A.	Modified closed	2*

NOTE: An asterisk (*) next to the number of amendments indicates bills that include only those amendments that were related to women's issues N.A. = not applicable. The 104th Congress subcommittees are as follows:

Agriculture:
Department Operations, Nutrition, and Foreign Agriculture (DONFA)
Appropriations:
Labor, Health and Human Services, Education and Related Agencies (LHHS)
Commerce, Justice, State (CJS)
District of Columbia (DC)
Foreign Operations (FO)
Treasury, Postal Service, and General Government (TPSGG)
Banking and Financial Services:
Housing and Community Opportunity (HCO)
Economic and Educational Opportunities:
Early Childhood, Youth, and Families (ECYF)
Employer-Employee Relations (EER)
Postsecondary Education, Training, and Life-Long Learning (PETLL)
Workforce Protections (WP)

(continued)

Table B2   (continued)

Commerce:
Commerce, Trade, and Hazardous Materials (CTHM)
Courts and Intellectual Property (CIP)
Health and Environment (HE)
Telecommunications and Finance (TF)
Government Reform and Oversight:
Government Management, Information and Technology (GMIT)
International Relations:
Human Rights (H Rts.)
Judiciary:
Commercial and Administrative Law (CAL)
Constitution (Const)
Crime
Immigration and Claims (IC)
National Security:
Military Personnel (MP)
Veterans' Affairs:
Hospitals and Health Care (HHC)
Ways and Means:
Health
Human Resources (HR)
Oversight (OV)

Chapter 1

1. EMILY's List is the most successful fundraiser among the groups devoted to the election of women candidates. While EMILY's List raised more than $20 million in the 2000 election cycle, WISH List raised $608,273 and the Susan B. Anthony List raised $25,995 (Federal Election Commission 2001a).

2. This book focuses on the connection between descriptive and substantive representation, i.e., whether electing women has an impact on the content of the policy agenda and outcomes. Proponents of descriptive representation also claim that the need for more women in office is a simple matter of justice and equality. Additionally, these theorists maintain that groups that have been excluded from politics require representatives to serve as role models and establish legitimacy for the group's participation in politics (Sapiro 1981; Phillips 1991, 1995, 1998; Mansbridge 1999).

3. Personal interview, August 18, 1999.

4. Another limitation of roll-call vote analyses is that they cannot provide an accurate depiction of the range of preferences in the legislature because they represent a censored sample in which legislators' choices are limited to the options placed in front of them by the committees and the House leadership.

5. Reingold (2000) addresses the importance of partisanship in her study of the California and Arizona state legislatures. However, she does not evaluate the impact of institutional position. Bratton and Haynie (1999) consider partisanship and committee membership but do not account for legislators with leadership positions on the committees.

6. Feminist scholars have recognized the important differences between sex, a biological category, and gender, a social construct derived from the cultural norms and institutions of a society. Additionally, gender differences often reflect hierarchies of power as the prevailing cultural norms reinforce the dominance of ideas and values associated with masculinity over those associated with femininity (Duerst-Lahti and Kelly 1995; Carver 1996; Reingold 2000; Durest-Lahti 2002).

7. This number includes the delegate from Washington, D. C., Eleanor Holmes Norton (D).

8. Through parental rights legislation, Christian conservatives hoped to prevent their children from being exposed to what they believe are immoral

influences. They wanted parents to have access to any records concerning their children as well as a requirement of parental approval for participation in surveys such as those concerning sexual behavior or substance abuse.

9. During the committee markup, members of the committee offer amendments and make changes to a bill.

10. The twenty-eight interview subjects included eight members of Congress, five committee staffers, and fifteen personal staff. Among the eight representatives were two Democratic men, one liberal and one conservative; two Democratic women, one liberal and one moderate to liberal; two Republican men, one conservative and one moderate; and two moderate Republican women. The five committee staffers included four majority Republican staffers and one minority Democratic staffer. Among the fifteen personal staff, I interviewed seven Republican staffers and eight Democratic staffers. The personal staff included chiefs of staff, legislative directors, and legislative assistants with special responsibility for social welfare policies like health care and education. The Republican staffers included staff for two men, one moderate and one conservative and for five women, two conservative and three moderate. The Democratic staffers included staff for two liberal men and for six women, three liberals, two moderate to liberal, and one conservative. Four interview subjects were associated with three representatives who are racial minorities, one African-American and two Hispanics.

11. The two conservative Republican women are the exception to these rules. The 104th Congress marked the first time that staunchly conservative Republican women were elected to Congress; therefore, these women are the only members interviewed who did not serve in both the 103rd and 104th Congresses. Further, to gain insight into the question of whether conservative women will make women's issues a priority from an antifeminist point of view, in these two cases, I did not follow the criterion that a member had to be involved in women's issues.

12. The interviews were largely open-ended and ranged in time from twenty minutes to one and a half hours. All interviews began by asking the subject to identify the representative's top three priorities and how he or she became involved in those issues. Subsequent questions concerned general legislative strategy, such as how the legislator decides which bills to cosponsor. The remaining questions were tailored to the specific interview and concerned a particular bill or policy area in which the member was involved. Questions directly related to the impact of women were not asked until the end of the interview and were not directly addressed in every case. The interviews were conducted between June 30 and September 29, 1999, in Washington, D.C.

13. Throughout the book, all unattributed quotes are from these interviews.

Chapter 2

1. Jennifer Dunn (R-WA) ran for majority leader in the 106th Congress, but she was defeated by the incumbent majority leader, Dick Armey (R-TX) (Katz and Doherty 1998). In the Senate, Margaret Chase Smith's tenure as chair of the Republican Conference (1967–72) represents the highest party leadership post attained by a woman in the Senate (Foerstel 2001b).

2. Green chaired the Subcommittee on Higher Education. Other congress-women have chaired various subcommittees, and several women have served as chairs of nonprestigious committees. In the period since the 1946 House Reorganization Act, six women have chaired full committees. Mary Teresea Norton (D-NJ) chaired the House Administration Committee from 1948 to her retirement in 1951. Prior to the 1946 reorganization of the House, she chaired the District of Columbia Committee and the Labor Committee, a post from which she ushered through the important wages and hours bill, the Fair Labor Standards Act of 1938. Edith Nourse Rogers (R-MA) chaired the Veterans Affairs Committee during the 80th Congress (1947–49); Leonor Sullivan (D-MO) chaired the Merchant Marine and Fisheries Committee in the 93rd and 94th Congresses (1973–77); and Pat Schroeder (D-CO) chaired the Select Committee on Children, Youth and Families in the 102nd Congress (1991–93); the House, however, eliminated select committees in the 103rd Congress (Gertzog 1995; Kaptur 1996). In the 104th Congress, Jan Meyers (R-KS) chaired the Small Business Committee and Nancy Johnson (R-CT) chaired the Standards of Official Conduct Committee, which handles ethics complaints. Also in the 104th Congress, Senator Nancy Landon Kassebaum (R-KS) chaired the Senate's Labor and Human Resources Committee (Congressional Quarterly Press 1996b).

3. Personal interview, July 6, 1999.

4. Pelosi's campaign for whip was unusually long because Democrats hoping to regain the majority in the 2000 elections assumed that the whip position would be open when the current whip David Bonior (D-MI) ascended to majority leader. When Bonior announced in July 2001 that he was retiring to run for governor, Pelosi and her opponent, Steny Hoyer (D-MD), resumed the campaign (Foerstel 2001a, 2001b).

5. The size of the gender gap varies depending on the source of the data. Carroll (1999) cites an eleven-point gap based on Voter News Service exit polls, while Kaufmann and Petrocik (1999) cite a fourteen-point gender gap based on the results of the National Election Study.

6. The choice of who will deliver the opposition's response to the State of the Union Address is always made with an eye toward public relations and who can best sell the party's programs to the American people. For example, in the 2000 Republican Response, Senator Bill Frist, as the Senate's only doctor, could reassure the public that the Republicans are protecting the people's interests in the debate over managed-care reform.

Chapter 3

1. This information is based on interviews with members and personal and committee staff associated with the bill.

2. I created the women's issue bill database from the monthly *Action Alerts* of the American Association of University Women (1993, 1994b, 1995, 1996b), the monthly *Legislative Updates* of the National Organization for Women (1993–96), the monthly "On the Hill" section of Concerned Women for America's *Family Voice* (1993, 1994, 1995, 1996), Eagle Forum's monthly *Phyllis Schlafly Report* (1993–96), the Congressional Caucus for Women's Issues' *Update: On Women and Family Issues* for the 103rd Congress, and the publications of Women's Policy, Inc., on the 104th Congress.

3. The synopses and summaries of action for the more than five thousand bills per Congress were obtained from Congressional Universe Bill Tracking Reports 103rd and 104th Congresses (1993–96). Similar information can be obtained by searching the Library of Congress Web site (thomas.loc.gov).

4. In the area of health, there were 254 additional bills sponsored on various aspects of health reform that are not included in the sample. This large number of health bills is most likely due to the consideration of President Clinton's health reform plan during the 103rd Congress. I felt that if I included all of these bills, the sample would be too cumbersome and skewed toward health issues and would not provide a measure of general interest in health issues. I chose instead to maintain the major health reform bills identified by the women's groups. I added only bills concerning long-term care insurance, nurses' services, and children's health, which matched the subjects of bills already identified by the women's groups. Thus, the health care index should not be interpreted as a definitive measure of interest in health bills. Similarly, after matching bills for the 104th Congress to the subject areas identified by the women's groups, I did not include an additional 137 health bills in the 104th Congress sample.

5. These patterns reflect more than the simple increase in membership that comes with majority status. For example, while only ten more Democratic men sponsored bills in the 103rd Congress, Democratic men as a group sponsored forty-seven more bills in the 103rd Congress than they sponsored in the 104th Congress. Similarly, an increase of forty-two Republican men sponsoring women's issue bills in the 104th Congress resulted in the sponsorship of 108 more women's issue bills by Republican men as a group.

6. Using Poole and Rosenthal's DW-NOMINATE scores, I determined that Linda Smith (R-WA) was the least conservative of the six conservative female freshmen. Using her ideology score as a baseline, I compared the bill sponsorship activity of freshman and nonfreshman Republicans with ideology scores greater than or equal to Smith's.

7. This provision was a priority of social conservatives who oppose the practice of surveying students on such issues as sexual behavior and drug use. The bill, entitled the Family Reinforcement Act, also included social welfare provisions including tax credits for adoption and the care of an elderly family member as well as a feminist proposal concerning minimum sentencing guidelines for sex offenders. Since the bill was part of the Contract with America, it is unclear how involved Vucanovich was in the planning of any individual provisions or how she became the member assigned to sponsor the bill.

8. There are 433 representatives included in the 103rd Congress sample and 430 representatives in the 104th Congress sample. The Speaker of the House was excluded because he generally does not sponsor legislation. All delegates, except the delegate from Washington, D.C., Eleanor Holmes Norton, are excluded because census information on district characteristics is only available for Washington, D.C., and Congress has a special responsibility for the District. Members who did not serve at least three-fourths of the term were dropped except for William Natcher in the 103rd Congress because he played a pivotal role in women's issue legislation as chairman of the Appropriations Committee and the Labor, Health and Human Services, and Education Subcommittee.

9. Ordered logit is the most appropriate model because, as shown in table 1, most representatives do not sponsor a women's issue bill. Therefore all the

dependent variables are skewed toward zero, and the critical decision is not how many women's issue bills members sponsor but whether they sponsor a women's issue bill at all. The employment of negative binomial event count models to dependent variables measuring the actual number of women's issue bills sponsored by each member revealed no significant differences in the regression results, thus verifying the appropriateness of the ordered logit models (King 1989; Long 1997).

10. Party affiliation and ideology are highly correlated, with a correlation coefficient of .9 in the 103rd Congress and .93 in the 104th Congress. This high level of correlation creates problems of multicolinearity. However, the fact that the ideology coefficient is often significant in the presence of the gender-party variables indicates that the inclusion of both variables allows one to capture differences in the behavior of liberals and conservatives within the two parties. The ideology variable is also correlated with the district variables and therefore reduces the impact of these variables. However, since the impact of gender is the main focus of the study, the ideology variable is always included to insure that differences attributed to gender are not better explained by a member's ideology.

11. I obtained the census data from U.S. Bureau of the Census (1993, 1995). The district votes for Clinton and Perot and the race and religion variables were identified using *Congressional Quarterly's Politics in America 1994: The 103rd Congress* (Duncan 1993) and *Congressional Quarterly's Politics in America 1996: The 104th Congress* (Duncan and Lawrence 1995).

12. Since most African-American and Hispanic representatives are elected from districts with high minority populations, the variables for minority representatives are highly correlated with the district variables. This high correlation often created problems with multicolinearity, and in these cases, the variable for the individual representative was dropped in favor of the more discriminating district variables. The religion variable identifies Catholic and Mormon representatives. Since it is not possible to identify which members are Christian fundamentalists, a group that expanded in the 104th Congress, the impact of the variable is probably dampened.

13. See app. A for a more detailed explanation of the development of the committee and subcommittee variables.

14. The models in tables 4 and 5 are optimized using Log Likelihood Ratio tests. The proportionate reduction in error (PRE) statistic indicates how much better the model predicts than if one were to just guess the mode. In all cases except the full set of women's issue bills for the 104th Congress, the mode is 0 because representatives do not generally sponsor women's issue bills of any kind. Thus, the models are explaining what factors influence a legislator to sponsor a women's issue bill. For the PRE $\pm$ 1, those who sponsor one bill, but are predicted as sponsoring two bills, are considered correct predictions. However, those who sponsor one bill and are predicted as sponsoring zero bills are not counted as correct predictions.

15. Party and ideology are more than 90 percent correlated in both the 103rd and 104th Congresses. The correlation between being a Democrat and the 1992 district vote for Clinton is 52 percent in the 103rd Congress and 61 percent in the 104th Congress. Despite these high correlations, the party and ideology variables are picking up separate effects. The large and negative coefficient for ideology indicates that the more positive the ideology score, indicating a more

conservative member, the less likely it is that the member will sponsor a women's issue bill. Once the ideological component is accounted for, the coefficients for Republican men and women are now accounting for the activities of party moderates.

16. One surprising result is the consistently negative, although generally insignificant, impact on women's issue bill sponsorship of representing a district with a higher percentage of African-Americans. However, the percentage of African-Americans in the district is highly correlated with ideology and the Democratic vote in the district, as represented by the percentage of the district voting for President Clinton. Thus, when the ideology and Clinton vote variables are excluded from the models, the district's African-American population is a positive and significant influence on women's issue bill sponsorship.

17. In separate models (not shown), a seat on a full committee that considered women's issue legislation had a positive influence on sponsorship. However, the impact of committee membership was reduced or became negative when subcommittee variables were added.

18. In this chapter and throughout the book, predicted probabilities are calculated using *Clarify: Software for Interpreting and Presenting Statistical Results* (Tomz, Wittenberg, and King 2001). The program runs a thousand simulations in which the variables of interest are allowed to vary and all other variables are set to their means (King, Tomz, and Wittenberg 2000). In this case, I varied the values of the gender-party, ideology, and district vote for Clinton coefficients and set the other independent variables to their means. To categorize a member as a liberal or conservative Democrat, and a moderate or conservative Republican, the DW-NOMINATE ideology scores were set at the 25 percent and 75 percent quartile values within each party. Similarly, to identify a member as representing a district with a high or low level of Democratic support in comparison with other members of his or her party, the district vote for Clinton was set at the 25 percent and 75 percent quartile values within each party. Among Democrats in the 103rd Congress, a high district vote for Clinton is 55 percent and a low district vote is 41 percent. Among Republicans, a high district vote for Clinton is 40 percent and a low district vote is 32 percent. Among Democrats in the 104th Congress, a high district vote for Clinton is 58.5 percent and a low district vote is 42 percent. Among Republicans a high district vote for Clinton is 41 percent and a low district vote for Clinton is 33 percent. The graphs do not compare, e.g., probabilities for conservative Democratic men or women from districts with a high level of Democratic support because it is reasonable to assume that a highly Democratic district would not elect a conservative. The range of probabilities in the graph provides an accurate representation of the types of members serving in Congress. The probabilities reported in figs. 3–5 represent the mean probability that a given representative will sponsor a women's issue, feminist, or social welfare bill.

Chapter 4

1. The number of feminist bills cosponsored ranges from zero to sixty-two bills in the 103rd Congress and zero to sixty bills in the 104th Congress. Representatives cosponsored from zero to fifty-one social welfare bills in the 103rd Congress and zero to sixty-two social welfare bills in the 104th Congress. Finally,

the number of antifeminist bills cosponsored ranges from zero to seven bills in the 103rd Congress and zero to fourteen bills in the 104th Congress.

2. Poole and Rosenthal's DW-NOMINATE scores are used to divide party members into ideological groups. The scores range from −1, indicating most liberal, to +1, indicating most conservative. Given the increasing ideological polarization of the parties throughout the 1990s, Republicans with DW-NOMINATE scores in the lower 30 percent of the Republican Party Caucus are characterized as moderate. Similarly, Democrats with DW-NOMINATE scores in the highest 30 percent of the Democratic Party Caucus are characterized as conservative. The remaining 70 percent of the legislators within each party are characterized as conservative Republicans and liberal Democrats.

3. The Defense of Marriage Act prohibits gay marriage while the Employment Nondiscrimination Act would prohibit employment discrimination on the basis of sexual orientation.

4. The requirement for parental permission to participate in surveys was favored by social conservatives who opposed adolescent participation in surveys about such issues as sexual activity and drug abuse. The bill also contained less ideological social welfare provisions including tax credits for adoption and the care of elderly family members and a feminist provision concerning minimum sentencing guidelines for sex offenders.

5. Sixteen Democratic men cosponsored the Partial Birth Abortion Act. Eleven Democratic men and one conservative Democratic woman cosponsored the Defense of Marriage Act. Two conservative Democratic women cosponsored an alternative to the Partial Birth Abortion Act. The alternative bill was designed to try to achieve a compromise between the pro-life and pro-choice forces by including an exception for both the life and health of the mother. However, the proposal failed to gain support from either the pro-choice or pro-life contingents.

6. The most common event count model is the Poisson regression model. This model assumes that the probability of an event occurring at any given time is constant within a specified period and independent of all previous events. However, members who cosponsor one bill on women's issues may be more likely to cosponsor additional bills on women's issues, thus violating the assumption of independence. The negative binomial model accounts for this dependence through the dispersion parameter. A dispersion parameter of 0 indicates an absence of dispersion and independence of events while a dispersion parameter that is greater than 0 indicates overdispersion (King 1989; Balla and Nemacheck 1999). When I estimated Poisson models for each of the dependent variables, χ^2 tests indicated that the dependent variables are not Poisson distributed and that the negative binomial is the more appropriate model.

7. There is not sufficient variation among the antifeminist bills to warrant further regression analysis.

8. For the feminist and social welfare models, the tables report the number of members whose cosponsorship behavior is predicted within one and two bills because there is less variation in these dependent variables than in the full set of women's issue bills.

9. As in chap. 3 and throughout the book, predicted probabilities are calculated using *Clarify: Software for Interpreting and Presenting Statistical Results* (Tomz,

Wittenberg, and King 2001). The probabilities reported in this chapter represent the mean probability that a given representative will cosponsor a women's issue, feminist, or social welfare bill. The methods used to calculate these predicted probabilities are similar to those described in chap. 3, n. 16.

10. In the 103rd Congress, liberal Democratic women in highly Democratic districts are predicted to cosponsor the most social welfare bills of any category of members: an average of seventeen social welfare bills compared to fourteen bills by similarly situated liberal Democratic men. In the 104th Congress, moderate Republican women are predicted to cosponsor the largest number of social welfare bills in comparison to any other category of members: an average of eighteen social welfare bills compared to, e.g., sixteen bills by liberal Democratic women and 14.5 bills by moderate Republican men.

Chapter 5

1. This number includes some legislation that was not originally included in the women's issue bill sample. For instance, several appropriations bills that generally did not concern women's issues attracted legislative riders concerning abortion. For example, in the 104th Congress, the defense appropriations bills included amendments concerning the use of private funds to obtain abortions at military hospitals.

2. The bill status reports for the 103rd and 104th Congresses (1993–96) from the Internet service LEGI-SLATE (www.legislate.com) provide detailed information on the amendments offered during committee markup and floor debate. This service has been purchased by OnCongress.CQ.com (www.cq.com). Researchers can also get markup data from the individual committees. To identify the women's issue amendments and characterize amendments as social welfare, feminist, and antifeminist, I also utilized the descriptions of committee debates in the 1993–96 *Congressional Quarterly Almanacs* (Congressional Quarterly Press 1994a, 1995a, 1996a, 1997) and the interest group reports from the women's groups, including the monthly *Action Alert* of the American Association of University Women (1993, 1994b, 1995, 1996b), the monthly *Legislative Updates* of the National Organization for Women (1993–96), the monthly "On the Hill" section of Concerned Women for America's *Family Voice* (1993, 1994, 1995, 1996), Eagle Forum's *Phyllis Schlafly Report* (1993–96), the Congressional Caucus for Women's Issues' *Update on Women and Family Issues* for the 103rd Congress, and the publications of Women's Policy, Inc., on the 104th Congress.

3. The overwhelming majority of committee amendments were first-degree amendments. In the 103rd Congress, members offered 422 first-degree amendments, seventeen second-degree amendments, and eight procedural amendments. During the 104th Congress, representatives offered 534 first-degree amendments, seventeen second-degree amendments, and thirty-seven procedural amendments. Appendix B explains the nature of the amendments that make up these categories.

4. At first glance, it may appear odd that the percentage of women's issue amendments sponsored by Republican men in the 103rd Congress is less than that in the 104th, while the absolute number of women's issue amendments sponsored by Republican men is greater in the 103rd Congress. However, the greater number of amendments sponsored by Republican men in the 103rd

Congress is due to the consideration of the Clinton Health Reform Bill. This comprehensive initiative was considered by eight committees and attracted 219 amendments. Republicans were strongly opposed to this bill and used it as a symbol to help them capture the majority in the 1994 elections. Republican men who served on the subcommittees with primary jurisdiction over the bill and the ranking minority members of these subcommittees and the full committee were particularly active in their efforts to amend the bill. For example, as ranking minority member of the Education and Labor Committee, Bill Goodling (R-PA) offered eighteen amendments to the Clinton Health Reform Bill and the bill reauthorizing the Elementary and Secondary Education Act. By contrast, in the 104th Congress, as chairman of the Education and Workforce Committee, Goodling proposed only five women's issue amendments. In the 104th Congress, only four Republican men offered more than five amendments, while in the 103rd Congress, eleven Republican men proposed more than five women's issue amendments.

5. Marge Roukema (R-NJ) offered an amendment to the Clinton health reform bill that would prohibit illegal aliens from receiving Women, Infants, and Children Nutrition Program (WIC) benefits and Susan Molinari (R-NY) tried to attach an amendment to the National Service Bill that would remove health and child-care benefits as well as the living stipend from the package of benefits that would be given to Americorps volunteers.

6. Two of the four conservative male freshmen that offered antifeminist floor amendments sought to amend bills that were not considered by the committees on which they served.

7. The dependent variables measure whether a legislator sponsored 0, 1, or 2 or more women's issue, feminist, or social welfare amendments. Ordered logit is the most appropriate model because, as shown in table 10, most members do not sponsor a women's issue amendment of any kind. Thus, in the 103rd Congress, only 126 members sponsored a women's issue amendment, leaving 307 representatives who did not sponsor any women's issue amendments. Accordingly, all the dependent variables are skewed toward zero and the critical decision is not how many women's issue amendments a member sponsors but whether they propose one at all. The models are optimized using log likelihood ratio tests.

8. The PRE ± 1 is calculated like a PRE for a logit model. If a representative is predicted as sponsoring an amendment, it is considered a correct prediction. Thus, those who sponsor one amendment, but are predicted as sponsoring two amendments, are considered correct predictions. However, those who sponsor one amendment and are predicted as sponsoring zero amendments are not counted as correct predictions.

9. Indeed, in a model that excluded, from the dependent variable, the amendments to the Clinton Health Reform Bill—the bill that received the most attention from the news media and interest groups—the coefficient for Democratic women is a positive and significant determinant of which members initiate women's issue amendments. I also created committee models that included a variable for those members who are on the committee but not the relevant subcommittee. These models reflected similar results to those in table 12. However, these models are essentially predicting those who sponsor committee amendments by the fact that they hold a seat on the committee, a rather circular

argument. Finally, I tested another model that included only those representatives who held a seat on one of the committees that considered the most women's issue bills. This model, however, reduced the variation in the dependent variable by excluding some members who offer women's issue amendments. It also excludes most of the women in Congress, since the majority did not hold seats on the committees and subcommittees with jurisdiction over the most women's issue legislation.

10. Personal interviews, July 6 and September 21, 1999.

11. As described in chap. 3, I utilized *Clarify: Software for Interpreting and Presenting Statistical Results* (Tomz, Wittenberg, and King 2001) to calculate the predicted probabilities. The probabilities reported in figs. 6–8 represent the mean probability that a given representative will offer a women's issue amendment in committee or a feminist amendment in committee or on the floor.

12. The level of district support for Democrats is measured by the district vote for Bill Clinton in 1992. To categorize a member as representing a district with a high or low level of support for Democrats given his or her party affiliation, the Clinton vote was set at the 25 percent or 75 percent quartile within each party. Among Democrats, a high district vote for Clinton is 58.5 percent and a low district vote is 42 percent. Among Republicans, a high district vote for Clinton is 41 percent and a low district vote for Clinton is 33 percent.

13. This account of Johnson's actions is based on interviews (July 6–7 and August 18, 1999) with staffers and members who participated in crafting the Welfare Reform Bill, as well as a review of the committee markup debate transcript.

14. During the 104th Congress, Jan Meyers (R-KS) chaired the Small Business Committee. In the Senate, Nancy Landon Kassebaum (R-KS) chaired the Labor and Human Resources Committee where she made the Health Insurance Portability Act the centerpiece of her legislative legacy (see Dodson 1997).

Chapter 6

1. To identify the amendments offered during floor debate, I used Congressional Universe's bill tracking reports (web.lexis-nexis.com/congcomp) for the 103rd and 104th Congresses (1993–96) and LEGI-SLATE's (www.legislate.com) bill status reports for the 103rd and 104th Congresses. LEGI-SLATE has been purchased by OnCongress.CQ.com (www.cq.com). Researchers can find similar information on the Library of Congress Web site (thomas.loc.gov). I characterized amendments as related to women's issues by reviewing the content of the amendment and consulting the descriptions of the floor debates in the 1993–96 *Congressional Quarterly Almanacs* (Congressional Quarterly Press 1994a, 1995a, 1996a, 1997) and the legislative reports from the women's groups, including the monthly *Action Alert* of the American Association of University Women, (1993, 1994b, 1995, 1996b) the monthly *Legislative Updates* of the National Organization for Women (1993–96), the monthly "On the Hill" section of Concerned Women for America's *Family Voice* (1993, 1994, 1995, 1996), Eagle Forum's *Phyllis Schlafly Report* (1993–96), the Congressional Caucus for Women's Issues' *Update on Women and Family Issues* for the 103rd Congress, and the publications of Women's Policy, Inc., on the 104th Congress. As with the committee analysis, the floor amendment sample also includes women's issue amendments

identified by the interest groups that were attached to bills not included in the original women's issue bill sample. Many of these amendments are legislative riders to appropriations bills. In both the 103rd and 104th Congresses, the floor debate on appropriations bills served as a battleground for pro-life and pro-choice forces over the issue of abortion. For example, legislators battled over amendments prohibiting funding for international family planning programs in the foreign operations appropriations bills and amendments to the defense appropriations bills prohibiting the use of private funds to obtain abortions on military bases.

2. Bills that pass by voice vote are also noncontroversial bills that are not amended. The two bills brought to the floor as privileged legislation were appropriations bills. Appropriations bills can get direct access to the floor because they must pass to keep the government running. By designating the legislation as privileged without a specific rule, members can offer unlimited amendments to the bill and the bill is subject to points of order (Oleszek 1996).

3. In the 103rd Congress, representatives offered 107 first-degree amendments, sixteen second-degree amendments, and 103 procedural amendments. In the 104th Congress, legislators sponsored 164 first-degree amendments, four second-degree amendments, and seventy-eight procedural amendments.

4. In the 103rd Congress, fifteen members sponsored twenty feminist amendments, fifty-two members sponsored ninety-two social welfare amendments, and fourteen members sponsored twenty antifeminist amendments. In the 104th Congress, thirty-three members sponsored forty-six feminist amendments, ninety members sponsored 140 social welfare amendments, and thirteen members sponsored seventeen antifeminist amendments. The number of amendments does not correspond to the total number of women's issue amendments in each Congress because some of the procedural amendments that do not include substantive content or a policy direction are not included in these categories. For example, motions to suspend the rules and pass a bill were not included in any of these categories.

5. In a separate model, a variable measuring those members who were on the full committee but not the women's issue subcommittee had a positive influence on the likelihood of sponsoring a women's issue floor amendment. However, the variable was always insignificant. To avoid overstating the importance of committee and subcommittee leaders, I ran additional models that excluded amendments to suspend the rules and pass the bill. Committee leaders generally offer these procedural amendments. The results of these regression models were substantially the same as those reported in this chapter.

6. The Speaker of the House is not included in the variable measuring majority party leaders because the Speaker generally does not offer amendments on the floor.

7. As described in chap. 3, n. 16, I utilized *Clarify: Software for Interpreting and Presenting Statistical Results* (Tomz, Wittenberg, and King 2001) to calculate the predicted probabilities. The probabilities reported in figs. 9 and 10 represent the mean probability that a given representative will offer a women's issue amendment on the floor.

8. Appendix A details the subcommittees that comprise the woman's issue subcommittee variables employed in the floor amendment models for the 103rd and 104th Congresses.

9. As one of his first acts as president, George W. Bush reinstated the Mexico City policy prohibiting funding for international family planning organizations that perform abortions or lobby their government to allow abortions.

Chapter 7

1. The American Association of University Women is the only one of the major liberal-leaning women's groups to publish a comprehensive vote rating in both the 103rd and the 104th Congress (1994a, 1996a). At the end of the congressional session, the Congressional Caucus for Women's Issues, in the 103rd Congress, and Women's Policy, Inc., in the 104th Congress, published summaries of the important bills for women considered in each Congress (Congressional Caucus for Women's Issues 1994, no. 6; Women's Policy, Inc. 1996; Clemmitt, Primmer, and Simms 1997). Those bills that came to a roll-call vote and did not pass unanimously were included in the sample. However, in the 104th Congress the sample does not include all of the numerous abortion votes taken during the congressional session. To prevent a bias toward abortion legislation, I included roll-call votes on a cross section of the major abortion debates, such as votes concerning family planning, federal funding of abortion, late-term abortions, and embryo research.

2. The fourteen-vote sample for the 103rd Congress includes the National Service Program; the School-to-Work Opportunities Act; the Elementary and Secondary Education Act (ESEA); the Unsoeld Amendment to the ESEA concerning sex education; the National Institutes of Health Revitalization Act, which includes programs for a variety of women's health concerns ranging from breast cancer to contraceptives; the Columbia Hospital for Women Land Conveyance Act; the Freedom of Access to Abortion Clinic Entrances Act; the Family Planning Amendments Act of 1993; the Hyde Amendment concerning Medicaid funding of abortion to the Fiscal Year 1994 Labor, Health and Human Services, and Education Appropriations Bill; the Omnibus Crime Bill, which included the Violence against Women Act; the Molinari Motion to Instruct on the Crime Bill, which concerned the admissibility of previous sex offenses in trials; the Family and Medical Leave Act; the Federal Nutrition Programs Reauthorization Act, which included the Women, Infants, and Children Nutrition Programs; and the Small Business Administration Reauthorization Act, which established an Office of Women's Business Ownership.

3. The fifteen-vote sample for the 104th Congress includes the Dixon Motion to Recommit the Fiscal Year 1996 District of Columbia Appropriations Bill, which concerned school vouchers; the Bonior Motion to Recommit the Balanced Budget Downpayment Act, which attempted to increase education funding; the Fiscal Year 1996 Labor, Health, and Human Services and Education Appropriations Bill; the Lowey Amendment to the Fiscal Year 1997 Labor, Health and Human Services, and Education Bill, which increased funding for the Women's Educational Equity Act programs; the Riggs Amendment to the Portal to Portal Act of 1947, which raised the minimum wage; the Partial Birth Abortion Act; the Greenwood Amendment, which restored domestic family planning funding to the Fiscal Year 1996 Labor, Health and Human Services, and Education Appropriations Bill; the DeLauro Amendment to the Department of Defense Reauthorization Act of 1995, which would have lifted the ban on the use of private funds for

abortions at military hospitals; the Lowey Amendment to the Fiscal Year 1996 Omnibus Appropriations Bill, which concerned Medicaid funding of abortion; the Lowey Amendment to the Fiscal Year 1997 Labor, Health and Human Services and Education Appropriations Bill, which concerned eliminating the ban on fetal tissue research; the Smith Amendment to the Fiscal Year 1996 Foreign Operations Appropriations Bill, which concerned limiting international family-planning funding; the Defense of Marriage Act, which prohibited gay marriage; the Hostettler Amendment to the Fiscal Year 1996 District of Columbia Appropriations Bill, which repealed a District of Columbia law granting benefits to unmarried (including homosexual) couples; the Personal Responsibility Act of 1995; and the Personal Responsibility and Work Opportunity Act of 1996, the final welfare reform bill. The Personal Responsibility Acts of 1995 and 1996 represent essentially the same welfare reform bill. However, when the welfare reform bill came up for a vote in 1995, only eight Republicans and eight Democrats defected from their party's position on the bill. When the House voted on the 1996 welfare reform bill, President Clinton, concerned about his upcoming reelection race, reversed his opposition to the Republican welfare bill, and ninety-eight Democrats joined Republicans in voting to pass the legislation.

4. This figure (54 percent) is derived from dividing seven by thirteen. I also analyzed dependent variables in which members received a score of 0.5 if they did not vote on a bill. Thus, in the 103rd Congress, a member who voted in favor of ten bills and did not vote for two bills would receive a score of $(10 + 0.5 + 0.5)/14 = 79\%$. Another dependent variable counted nonvoters as missing variables, which in effect gave them a score of zero when the bills were summed and averaged across the total number of votes. For example, in the 103rd Congress, a member who voted for ten bills and did not cast a vote on two bills received a score of $10/14 = 71\%$. The results of the regression models using these dependent variables are not significantly different from the regression models reported in this chapter.

5. Between the 103rd and the 104th Congresses, liberal women's issue voting among Republican men dropped 26 percent, from a mean of 38 percent (5.3/14 bills) in the 103rd Congress to a mean of 12 percent (1.8/15 bills) in the 104th Congress. Liberal women's issue voting among Republican women dropped 47 percent, from a mean of 73 percent (10.2/14 bills) in the 103rd Congress to a mean of 26 percent (3.9/15 bills) in the 104th Congress.

6. Due to concern about heteroskedasticity in the residuals, I employed White's correction for heteroskedasticity. White's heteroskedastic consistent standard errors weight the standard error of the coefficients, thus reducing the probability that one will falsely reject the null hypothesis that the coefficient is truly zero. The R^2 statistic indicates how well the model fits the data; thus, the women's issue vote models in table 19 predict 78 percent of the variation in members' women's issue voting in the 103rd Congress and 90 percent of the variation in voting in the 104th Congress.

7. There are numerous internal-member congressional caucuses that bring together members who share an ideological viewpoint or a common interest in an issue. These caucuses vary in their levels of activity and influence within the political parties. Some, like the Tuesday Group (also known as the Tuesday Lunch Bunch) representing moderate Republicans and the Conservative Action

Team, gained regular seats at Republican Party leadership meetings in the 104th Congress. Within the Democratic Party, the Blue Dogs, representing conservative Democrats, the Congressional Black Caucus, and the Hispanic Caucus are powerful forces. Other caucuses, like the Children's Caucus, restrict themselves to information gathering and to holding educational forums for members. On the abortion issue, pro-choice forces are represented by the Pro-Choice Caucus, and in the 103rd and 104th Congresses, the Congressional Caucus for Women's Issues (CCWI). The CCWI adopted a pro-choice plank in the 103rd Congress, but they dropped it in the 106th Congress in an effort to make the caucus more bipartisan. On the pro-life side, the Family Caucus and the Values Action Team joined the Pro-Life Caucus in its lobbying efforts. (See Hammond [1997] and Kolodny [1999] for more information about congressional caucuses.)

8. Information about the power and tactics of the pro-life and pro-choice forces and their impact on the political parties was gathered from interviews with pro-choice and pro-life members and staff within both the Democratic and Republican parties (July 12, 16, 23, and 28, August 18, and September 29, 1999)

Chapter 8

1. Personal interviews with Democratic and Republican staff involved in the reauthorization of the Elementary and Secondary Education Act (July 14, August 11 and 18, and September 21, 1999).

Appendixes

1. When the Republicans ascended to the majority in the 104th Congress, they eliminated some committees and subcommittees, such as the Post Office and Civil Service Committee. They also changed the names of many committees and subcommittees to reflect Republican priorities. For example, the Education and Labor Committee became the Economic and Educational Opportunities Committee. To identify the membership of the various committees and subcommittees, I used Congressional Quarterly's *Players, Politics and Turf of the 103rd Congress* (1994b) and *Players, Politics and Turf of the 104th Congress* (1996b).

References

Aldrich, John H. 1995. *Why Parties? The Origin and Transformation of Political Parties in America.* Chicago: University of Chicago Press.

Aldrich, John, and David Rhode. 1995. "The Transition to Republican Rule in the House: Implications for Theories of Congressional Politics." Paper presented at the annual meeting of the American Political Science Association, Chicago, August 31–September 3.

————. 1997. "Balance of Power: Republican Party Leadership and the Committee System in the 104th House." Paper presented at the annual meeting of the Midwest Political Science Association, Chicago, April 10–13.

————. 2000. "The Republican Revolution and the House Appropriations Committee." *Journal of Politics* 62:1–33.

Alexander, Deborah, and Kristi Anderson. 1993. "Gender as a Factor in the Attribution of Leadership Traits." *Political Research Quarterly* 46:527–45.

American Association of University Women. 1993. *Action Alert,* vol. 13, nos. 1–11.

————. 1994a. "AAUW Voting Record, 103rd Congress." *AAUW Outlook* (fall).

————. 1994b. *Action Alert,* vol. 14, nos. 1–11.

————. 1995. *Action Alert,* vol. 15, nos. 1–12.

————. 1996a. "AAUW Voting Record, 104th Congress." *AAUW Outlook* (fall).

————. 1996b. *Action Alert,* vol. 16, nos. 1–12.

Andersen, Kristi. 1997. "Gender and Public Opinion." In *Understanding Public Opinion,* edited by Barbara Norrander and Clyde Wilcox. Washington D.C.: Congressional Quarterly, Inc.

Arnold, Douglas. 1990. *The Logic of Congressional Action.* New Haven, Conn.: Yale University Press.

Baker, Paula. 1984. "The Domestication of Politics: Women and American Political Society, 1780–1920." *American Historical Review* 89:620–47.

Balla, Steven J., and Christine L. Nemacheck. 1999. "Position Taking, Legislative Signaling, and Non-Expert Extremism: Cosponsorship of Managed Care Legislation in the 105th House of Representatives." Paper presented at the annual meeting of the Midwest Political Science Association, Chicago, April 15–17.

Berkman, Michael B., and Robert E. O'Connor. 1993. "Do Women Legislators Matter? Female Legislators and State Abortion Policy." *American Politics Quarterly* 21:102–24.

Biersack, Robert, and Paul S. Herrnson. "Political Parties and the Year of the Woman." In *The Year of the Woman: Myths and Realities*, edited by Elizabeth Adel Cook, Sue Thomas, and Clyde Wilcox. Boulder, Colo.: Westview Press.

Bingham, Clara. 1997. *Women on the Hill: Challenging the Culture of Congress.* New York: Time Books.

Boxer, Barbara. 1994. *Strangers in the Senate.* Washington, D.C.: National Press Books.

Bratton, Kathleen A., and Kerry L. Haynie. 1999. "Agenda Setting and Legislative Success in State Legislatures: The Effects of Gender and Race." *Journal of Politics* 61:658–79.

Brown, Peter A., and Howard Scripps. 1994. "White Male Voters Receptive to GOP Message." *Cleveland Plain Dealer*, 27 November, 8A.

Bruni, Frank. 1999. "Three Democratic Women Lead on Gun Control." *New York Times*, 14 June, A18.

Burnham, Walter Dean. 1970. *Critical Elections and the Mainsprings of American Politics.* New York: W. W. Norton & Co.

Burrell, Barbara C. 1994. *A Woman's Place Is in the House: Campaigning for Congress in the Feminist Era.* Ann Arbor: University of Michigan Press.

Canon, David T. 1999. *Race, Redistricting, and Representation.* Chicago: University of Chicago Press.

Carmines Edward C., and James A. Stimson. 1989. *Issue Evolution: Race and the Transformation of American Politics.* Princeton, N.J.: Princeton University Press.

Carney, Dan. 1999. "Beyond Guns and Violence: A Battle for House Control." *Congressional Quarterly Weekly Report*, 19 June, 1426–32.

Carroll, Susan J. 1999. "The Disempowerment of the Gender Gap: Soccer Moms and the 1996 Elections." *PS: Political Science and Politics* 32:7–11.

———. 2002. "Representing Women: Congresswomen's Perception of Their Representational Roles." In *Women Transforming Congress*, edited by Cindy Simon Rosenthal. Norman: University of Oklahoma Press, in press.

Carver, Terrell. 1996. *Gender Is Not a Synonym for Women.* Boulder, Colo.: Lynne Rienner Publishers.

Casey, Kathleen, and Susan Carroll. 1998. "Wyoming Wolves and Dead-Beat Dads: The Impact of Women Members of Congress on Welfare Reform." Paper presented at the annual meeting of the American Political Science Association, Boston, September 3–6.

Center for the American Woman and Politics. 1994. *Fact Sheet: Women in Elective Office 1994.* New Brunswick: Rutgers—The State University of New Jersey, Center for the American Woman and Politics.

———. 2000. *Gender Gap in the 2000 Elections.* New Brunswick: Rutgers—The State University of New Jersey, Center for the American Woman and Politics.

Chaney, Carole K., R. Michael Alvarez, and Jonathan Nagler. 1998. "Explaining the Gender Gap in the U.S. Presidential Elections, 1980–1992." *Political Research Quarterly* 51:311–40.

Chaney, Carole, and Barbara Sinclair. 1994. "Women and the 1992 House Elections." In *The Year of the Woman: Myths and Realities*, edited by Elizabeth Adel Cook, Sue Thomas, and Clyde Wilcox. Boulder, Colo.: Westview Press.

Chodorow, Nancy. 1974. "Family Structure and Feminine Personality." In *Women, Culture, and Society*, edited by M. Z. Rosaldo and L. Lamphere. Stanford, Calif.: Stanford University Press.

Clark, Janet. 1998. "Women at the National Level: An Update on Roll Call Voting Behavior." In *Women and Elective Office: Past, Present, and Future*, edited by Sue Thomas and Clyde Wilcox. New York: Oxford University Press.

Clausen, Aage. 1973. *How Congressmen Decide: A Policy Focus*. New York: St. Martin's Press.

Clemmitt, Marcia, Leslie Primmer, and Marjorie Simms. 1997. *The Record: Gains and Losses for Women and Families in the 104th Congress*. Washington, DC: Women's Policy, Inc.

Concerned Women for America. 1993. "On the Hill." *Family Voice* (January–December).

———. 1994. "On the Hill." *Family Voice* (January–December).

———. 1995. "On the Hill." *Family Voice* (January–December).

———. 1996. "On the Hill." *Family Voice* (January–December).

Congressional Caucus for Women's Issues. 1993. *Update on Women and Family Issues in Congress*, vol. 13, nos. 1–10.

———. 1994. *Update on Women and Family Issues in Congress*, vol. 14, nos. 1–6.

Congressional Quarterly Press. 1994a. *Congressional Quarterly Almanac: 103rd Congress First Session 1993*. Washington, D.C.: Congressional Quarterly Press.

———. 1994b. *Players, Politics and Turf of the 103rd Congress*. Vol. 51, suppl. to no. 18. Washington, D.C.: Congressional Quarterly Press.

———. 1995a. *Congressional Quarterly Almanac: 103rd Congress Second Session, 1994*. Washington, D.C.: Congressional Quarterly Press.

———. 1995b. *Congressional Roll Call 1993: A Chronology and Analysis of Votes in the House and Senate, 103rd Congress, Second Session*. Washington, D.C.: Congressional Quarterly Press.

———. 1996a. *Congressional Quarterly Almanac: 104th Congress First Session, 1995*. Washington, D.C.: Congressional Quarterly Press.

———. 1996b. *Players, Politics and Turf of the 104th Congress*. Vol. 54, suppl. to no. 12. Washington, D.C.: Congressional Quarterly Press.

———. 1997. *Congressional Quarterly Almanac: 104th Congress Second Session, 1996*. Washington, D.C.: Congressional Quarterly Press.

Congressional Record. 106th Cong., 1st sess., 1999. Vol. 145.

Congressional Universe. 1993–96. Bill tracking reports, 103rd and 104th Congresses. Bethesda, Md.: Congressional Information Service. http://web.lexis-nexis.com/congcomp.

Conway, M. Margaret, David W. Ahern, and Gertrude A. Stevernagel. 1999. *Women and Public Policy: A Revolution in Progress*. 2d ed. Washington, D.C.: Congressional Quarterly Press.

Costain, Anne N. 1992. *Inviting Women's Rebellion: A Political Process Interpretation of the Women's Movement*. Baltimore: Johns Hopkins University Press.

Costello, Cynthia B., and Anne J. Stone, eds. 2001. *The American Woman, 2001–2002: Getting to the Top.* New York: W. W. Norton & Co., for the Women's Research and Education Institute.

Cox, Gary W., and Matthew D. McCubbins. 1993. *Legislative Leviathan: Party Government in the House.* Berkley: University of California Press.

Cramer Walsh, Katherine. 2002. "Resonating to Be Heard: Gendered Debate on the Floor of the House." In *Women Transforming Congress,* edited by Cindy Simon Rosenthal. Norman: University of Oklahoma Press, in press.

Dodson, Debra L., and Susan Carroll. 1991. *Reshaping the Agenda: Women in State Legislatures.* New Brunswick: Rutgers—The State University of New Jersey, Center for the American Woman and Politics.

Dodson, Debra L., et al. 1995. *Voices, Views, Votes: The Impact of Women in the 103rd Congress.* New Brunswick: Rutgers—The State University of New Jersey, Center for the American Woman and Politics.

Dodson, Debra L. 1997. "What a Difference an Election Makes: Representing Women's Interests on Health Care in the 104th Congress." Paper presented at the annual meeting of the American Political Science Association, Washington, D.C., August 28–31.

———. 1998. "Representing Women's Interests in the U.S. House of Representatives." In *Women and Elective Office: Past, Present, and Future,* edited by Sue Thomas and Clyde Wilcox. New York: Oxford University Press.

———. 2000. "Representation, Gender and Reproductive Rights in the U.S. Congress." Paper Presented at the Women Transforming Congress Conference, University of Oklahoma, Norman, April 13–15.

Dolan, Julie. 1997. "Support for Women's Interests in the 103rd Congress: The Distinct Impact of Congressional Women." *Women and Politics* 18:81–94.

Dolan, Kathleen. 2002. "Electoral Context, Issues, and Voting for Women in the 1990s." *Women and Politics,* vol. 23 (in press).

Dolan, Kathleen, and Lynn Ford. 1995. "Women in the State Legislatures: Feminist Identity and Legislative Behaviors." *American Politics Quarterly* 23:96–108.

Duerst-Lahti, Georgia. 2002. "Manliness, Ideology, and Congress as Governing Institution: Implications for Studying Women in Congress." In *Women Transforming Congress,* edited by Cindy Simon Rosenthal. Norman: University of Oklahoma Press, in press.

Duerst-Lahti, Georgia, and Rita Mae Kelly. 1995. "On Governance, Leadership, and Gender." In *Gender Power, Leadership, and Governance,* edited by Georgia Duerst-Lahti and Rita Mae Kelly. Ann Arbor: University of Michigan Press.

Duncan, Phil, ed. 1993. *Congressional Quarterly's Politics in America 1994: The 103rd Congress.* Washington, D.C.: Congressional Quarterly Press.

Duncan, Phil, and Christine Lawrence. 1995. *Congressional Quarterly's Politics in America 1996: The 104th Congress.* Washington, D.C.: Congressional Quarterly Press.

Earle, Geoff. 2000. "Democratic Whip Race off to Early Start." *National Journal's Congress Daily,* 24 January.

Edmonds, Patricia, and Richard Benedetto. 1994. "Angry White Men: Their Votes Turn the Tide for GOP." *USA Today,* 11 November, 1A.

Edsall, Thomas B. 2001. "RNC Plans Drive to Reach Female Voters; Training Programs, Web Site Unveiled." *Washington Post*, 20 July, A12.

Eilperin, Juliet. 2001. "House GOP Revamps Panels' Leadership." *Washington Post*, 5 January, A01.

Evans, C. Lawrence, and Walter Oleszek. 1997. *Congress under Fire: Reform Politics and the Republican Majority*. Boston: Houghton Mifflin Co.

Federal Election Commission. 2001a. "Committee Summary Reports." www.fec.gov.

———. 2001b. "Top 50 PAC's Receipts, 1999–2001." www.fec.gove/press/053101pacfund/tables/pacrec00.htm.

Fenno, Richard. 1973. *Congressmen in Committees*. Boston: Little Brown & Co., Inc.

———. 1978. *Home Style: House Members in Their Districts*. Boston: Little Brown & Co., Inc.

Fiorina, Morris. 1974. *Representatives, Roll Calls, and Constituencies*. Lexington, Mass.: Lexington Books.

Flammang, Janet A. 1997. *Women's Political Voice: How Women Are Transforming the Practice and Study of Politics*. Philadelphia: Temple University Press.

Flexner, Eleanor. 1975. *Century of Struggle: The Women's Rights Movement in the United States*. Cambridge, Mass.: Harvard University Press.

Foerstel, Karen. 2000a. "The Limits of Outreach." *Congressional Quarterly Weekly Report*, 11 November, 2649–51.

———. 2000b. "Choosing Chairmen: Tradition's Role Fades." *Congressional Quarterly Weekly Report*, 9 December, 2796–2801.

———. 2001. "Hoyer's and Pelosi's 3-Year Race for Whip: It's All Over but the Voting." *Congressional Quarterly Weekly Report*, 6 October, 2321–25.

———. 2001b. "Pelosi's Vote-Counting Prowess Earns Her the House Democrats' No. 2 Spot." *Congressional Quarterly Weekly Report*, 13 October, 2397–98.

Foerstel, Karen, and Herbert Foerstel. 1996. *Climbing the Hill: Gender Conflict in Congress*. Westport, Conn.: Praeger Publishers.

Foerstel, Karen, with Alan K. Ota. 2001. "Early Grief for GOP Leaders in New Committee Rules." *Congressional Quarterly Weekly Report*, 6 January, 10–14.

Fox, Richard Logan. 1997. *Gender Dynamics in Congressional Elections*. Thousand Oaks, Calif.: Sage Publications, Inc.

Frankovic, Kathleen A. 1977. "Sex and Voting in the U.S. House of Representatives, 1961–1975." *American Politics Quarterly* 5:315–30.

Gehlen, Freida. 1977. "Women Members of Congress: A Distinctive Role." In *A Portrait of Marginality: The Political Behavior of the American Woman*, edited by Marianne Githens and Jewell Prestage. New York: McKay Co.

Gelb, Joyce, and Marian Lief Palley. 1996. *Women and Public Policies: Reassessing Gender Politics*. Charlottesville: University Press of Virginia.

Gertzog, Irwin. 1995. *Congressional Women: Their Recruitment, Integration, and Behavior*. 2d ed. Westport, Conn.: Praeger Publishers.

Gilligan, Carol. 1982. *In a Different Voice: Psychological Theory and Women's Development*. Cambridge, Mass.: Harvard University Press.

Gimpel, James. 1996. *Fulfilling the Contract: The First Hundred Days*. Boston: Allyn & Bacon Co.

Greenberg, Anna. 1998. "Deconstructing the Gender Gap." Paper presented at the annual meeting of the Midwest Political Science Association, Chicago, April 23–26.

Greenblatt, Alan. 1997. "Ex-Rep Lincoln to Seek Bumpers' Senate Seat." *Congressional Quarterly Weekly Report*, 2 August, 1887.

Hall, Richard. 1996. *Participation in Congress.* New Haven, Conn.: Yale University Press.

Hall, Richard, and Frank Wayman. 1990. "Buying Time: Moneyed Interests and the Mobilization of Bias in Congressional Committees." *American Political Science Review* 84:797–820.

Hammond, Susan Webb. 1997. "Congressional Caucuses in the 104th Congress." In *Congress Reconsidered*, edited by Lawrence C. Dodd and Bruce I. Oppenheimer. 6th ed. Washington, D.C.: Congressional Quarterly Press.

Hardin, John. 1998. "An In-Depth Look at Congressional Committee Jurisdictions Surrounding Health Issues." *Journal of Health Politics, Policy and Law* 23:517–50.

Hartmann, Susan M. 1989. *From Margin to Mainstream: American Women and Politics since 1960.* New York: Alfred A. Knopf, Inc.

Huddy, Leonie, and Nayda Terkildsen. 1993a. "The Consequences of Gender Stereotypes for Women Candidates at Different Levels and Types of Offices." *Political Research Quarterly* 46:502–25.

———. 1993b. "Gender Stereotypes and the Perception of Male and Female Candidates." *American Journal of Political Science* 37:119–47.

Kanter, Rosabeth Moss. 1977. "Some Effects of Proportions on Group Life: Skewed Sex Ratios and Responses to Token Women." *American Journal of Sociology* 82:965–90.

Kaptur, Marcy. 1996. *Women of Congress: A Twentieth-Century Odyssey.* Washington, D.C.: Congressional Quarterly, Inc.

Kathlene, Lynn. 1994. "Power and Influence of State Legislative Policymaking: The Interaction of Gender and Position in Committee Hearing Debates." *American Political Science Review* 88:560–76.

———. 1995. "Alternative Views of Crime: Legislative Policymaking in Gendered Terms." *Journal of Politics* 57:696–723.

———. 1998. "In a Different Voice: Women and the Policy Process." In *Women and Elective Office: Past, Present, and Future*, edited by Sue Thomas and Clyde Wilcox. New York: Oxford University Press.

Katz, Jeffrey L. 1998. "GOP Must Decide How Much of Gingrich's Team to Keep." *Congressional Quarterly Weekly Report*, 14 November, 3057–61.

Katz, Jeffrey L., and Carroll J. Doherty. 1998. "New GOP Leaders' Watchword Is Realism Not Revolution." *Congressional Quarterly Weekly Report*, 21 November, 3161–66.

Kaufmann, Karen M., and John R. Petrocik. 1999. "The Changing Politics of American Men: Understanding the Sources of the Gender Gap." *American Journal of Political Science* 43:864–87.

Kessler, Daniel, and Keith Krehbiel. 1996. "Dynamics of Cosponsorship." *American Political Science Review* 90:555–66.

Kiewiet, D. Roderick, and Matthew McCubbins. 1991. *The Logic of Delegation: Congressional Parties and the Appropriations Process.* Chicago: University of Chicago Press.

Killian, Linda. 1998. *The Freshmen: What Happened to the Republican Revolution?* Boulder, Colo.: Westview Press.

King, David. 1997. *Turf Wars: How Congressional Committees Claim Jurisdiction.* Chicago: University of Chicago Press.

King, Gary. 1989. "Variance Specification in Event Count Models: From Restrictive Assumptions to a Generalized Estimator." *American Journal of Political Science* 33:762–84.

King, Gary, Michael Tomz, and Jason Wittenberg. 2000. "Making the Most of Statistical Analyses: Improving Interpretation and Presentation." *American Journal of Political Science* 44:341–55.

Kingdon, John W. 1989. *Congressmen's Voting Decisions.* 3d ed. Ann Arbor: University of Michigan Press.

Kirchhoff, Sue. 1999. "Dollars and Sensitivities: Finessing the Gender Gap." *Congressional Quarterly Weekly Report,* 24 April, 951–53.

Kolodny, Robin. 1999. "Moderate Success: Majority Status and the Changing Nature of Factionalism in the House Republican Party." In *New Majority or Old Minority? The Impact of Republicans on Congress,* edited by Nicol C. Rae and Colton C. Campbell. Lanham, Md.: Rowman & Littlefield Publishers.

Krehbiel, Keith. 1991. *Information and Legislative Organization.* Ann Arbor: University of Michigan Press.

———. 1995. "Cosponsors and Wafflers from A to Z." *American Journal of Political Science* 39:906–23.

———. 1998. *Pivotal Politics: A Theory of U.S. Lawmaking.* Chicago: University of Chicago Press.

Leader, Shelah Gilbert. 1977. "The Policy Impact of Elected Women Officials." In *The Impact of the Electoral Process,* edited by Joseph Cooper and Louis Maisel. Beverly Hills, Calif.: Sage Publications.

LEGI-SLATE. 1993–96. Bill status reports for 103rd and 104th Congresses. www.legislate.com. (This service was later purchased by Congressional Quarterly's OnCongress.CQ.com [www.cq.com].)

Levy, Dena, Charles Tien, and Rachelle Aved. 2002. "Do Differences Matter? Women Members of Congress and the Hyde Amendment." *Women and Politics,* vol. 23 (in press).

Lips, Hilary M. 1995. "Gender-Role Socialization: Lessons in Femininity." In *Women: A Feminist Perspective,* edited by Jo Freeman. 5th ed. Mountain View, Calif.: Mayfield Publishing.

Long, J. Scott. 1997. *Models for Categorical and Limited Dependent Variables.* Thousand Oaks, Calif.: Sage Publications.

Lublin, David. 1997. *The Paradox of Representation: Racial Gerrymander and Minority Interests in Congress.* Princeton, N.J.: Princeton University Press.

Maltzman, Forrest. 1995. "Meeting Competing Demands: Committee Performance in the Postreform House." *American Journal of Political Science* 39:653–82.

———. 1997. *Competing Principals: Committees, Parties, and the Organization of Congress.* Ann Arbor: University of Michigan Press.

Maltzman, Forrest, and Steven S, Smith. 1994. "The Multiple Principals and Motivations of Congressional Committees." *Legislative Studies Quarterly* 19:457–76.

Mansbridge, Jane. 1999. "Should Blacks Represent Blacks and Women Represent Women? A Contingent 'Yes.'" *Journal of Politics* 61:628–57.

Maraniss, David, and Michael Weisskopf. 1996. *"Tell Newt to Shut Up!"* New York: Simon & Schuster.

Margolies-Mezvinsky, Marjorie, with Barbara Feinman. 1994. *A Woman's Place ...: The Freshmen Women Who Changed the Face of Congress.* New York: Crown Publishers, Inc.

Marks, Peter. 2000. "Effort to Paint Gore as Conservative." *New York Times,* 24 February, A24.

Mayhew, David R. 1974. *Congress: The Electoral Connection.* New Haven, Conn.: Yale University Press.

McCarty, Nolan M., Keith T. Poole, and Howard Rosenthal. 1997. *Income Redistribution and the Realignment of American Politics.* Washington, D.C.: AEI Press.

McDermott, Monika L. 1997. "Voting Cues in Low-Information Elections: Candidate Gender as a Social Information Variable in Contemporary U.S. Elections." *American Journal of Political Science* 41:270–83.

Miller, Karen Czarnecki. 1995. "Will These Women Clean House." *Policy Review* 72:77–80.

Molinari, Susan, with Elinor Burkett. 1998. *Representative Mom: Balancing Budgets, Bill, and Baby in the U.S. Congress.* New York: Doubleday.

National Organization for Women. 1993–96. *Legislative Update* (February–December).

Nelson, Candice. 1994. "Women's PACs and the Year of the Woman." In *The Year of the Woman: Myths and Realities,* edited by Elizabeth Adell Cook, Sue Thomas, and Clyde Wilcox. Boulder, Colo.: Westview Press.

Norton, Noelle H. 1994. "Congressional Committee Power: The Reproductive Policy Inner Circle, 1969–1992." Ph.D. dissertation, University of California, Santa Barbara.

———. 1995. "Women, Its Not Enough to Be Elected: Committee Position Makes a Difference." In *Gender Power, Leadership, and Governance,* edited by Georgia Duerst-Lahti and Rita Mae Kelly. Ann Arbor: University of Michigan Press.

———. 1999. "Committee Influence over Controversial Policy: The Reproductive Policy Case." *Policy Studies Journal* 27:203–16.

———. 2002. "Transforming Congress from the Inside: Women in Committee." In *Women Transforming Congress,* edited by Cindy Simon Rosenthal. Norman: University of Oklahoma Press, in press.

Oleszek, Walter. 1996. *Congressional Procedures and the Policy Process.* 4th ed. Washington, D.C.: Congressional Quarterly Press.

Owens, John E. 1997. "The Return of Party Government in the U.S. House of Representatives: Central Leadership—Committee Relations in the 104th Congress." *British Journal of Political Science* 27:247–72.

Pearson, Kathryn L. 2001. "Legislating in Women's Interests? Congresswomen in the 106th Congress." Paper presented at the annual meeting of the American Political Science Association, San Francisco, August 30–September 2.

Phillips, Anne. 1991. *Engendering Democracy.* University Park: Pennsylvania State University Press.

———. 1995. *The Politics of Presence.* Oxford: Oxford University Press.

———. 1998. "Democracy and Representation: Or, Why Should It Matter Who Our Representatives Are?" In *Feminism and Politics,* edited by Anne Phillips. New York: Oxford University Press.

Phyllis Schlafly Report. 1993–96. (January–December).

Pitkin, Hanna Fenichel. 1967. *The Concept of Representation.* Berkley: University of California Press.

Poole, Keith T. 1988. "Recent Developments in Analytical Models of Voting in the U.S. Congress." *Legislative Studies Quarterly* 13:117–33.

Poole, Keith T., and R. Steven Daniels. 1985. "Ideology, Party, and Voting in the U.S. Congress, 1959–1980." *American Political Science Review* 79:373–99.

Poole, Keith T., and Howard Rosenthal. 1991. "Patterns of Congressional Voting." *American Journal of Political Science* 35:228–78.

———. 1997. *Congress: A Political-Economic History of Roll Call Voting.* New York: Oxford University Press.

Plutzer, Eric, and John Zipp. 1996. "Identity Politics, Partisanship, and Voting for Women Candidates." *Public Opinion Quarterly* 60:30–57.

Reingold, Beth. 1992. "Concepts of Representation among Female and Male State Legislators." *Legislative Studies Quarterly* 17:509–37.

———. 2000. *Representing Women: Sex, Gender, and Legislative Behavior in Arizona and California.* Chapel Hill: University of North Carolina Press.

Rhode, David W. 1991. *Parties and Leaders in the Postreform House.* Chicago: University of Chicago Press.

Rosenthal, Cindy Simon. 1997. "A View of Their Own: Women's Committee Leadership Styles and State Legislatures." *Policy Studies Journal* 25:585–600.

———. 1998. *When Women Lead: Integrative Leadership in State Legislatures.* New York: Oxford University Press.

Rossiter, Clinton, ed. 1961. *The Federalist Papers: Alexander Hamilton, James Madison, John Jay.* New York: Mentor Book.

Saint-Germain, Michelle A. 1989. "Does Their Difference Make a Difference? The Impact of Women on Public Policy in the Arizona Legislature." *Social Science Quarterly* 70:956–68.

Sanbonmatsu, Kira. 1997. "Democrats vs. Republicans: Gender Roles and the Gender Gap." Paper presented at the annual meeting of the American Political Science Association, Washington, D.C., August 28–31.

———. 2002. *Gender Equality, Political Parties, and the Politics of Women's Place.* Ann Arbor: University of Michigan Press, in press.

Sapiro, Virginia. 1981. "Research Frontier Essay: When Are Interests Interesting? The Problem of Political Representation of Women." *American Political Science Review* 75:701–16.

———. 1981–82. "If U.S. Senator Baker Were a Woman: An Experimental Study of Candidate Images." *Political Psychology* 2:61–83.

———. 1983. *The Political Integration of Women.* Chicago: University of Illinois Press.

Schiller, Wendy. 1995. "Senators as Political Entrepreneurs: Using Bill Sponsorship to Shape Legislative Agendas." *American Journal of Political Science* 39:186–203.

Schroedel Jean R., and Bruce Snyder. 1994. "Patty Murray: The Mom in Tennis Shoes Goes to the Senate." In *The Year of the Woman: Myths and Realities,* edited by Elizabeth Adel Cook, Sue Thomas, and Clyde Wilcox. Boulder, Colo.: Westview Press.

Seltzer, Richard, Jody Newman, and Melissa Voorhees Leighton. 1997. *Sex as a Political Variable: Women as Candidates and Voters in American Elections.* Boulder, Colo.: Lynne Rienner Publishers.

Shapiro, Robert, and Harpreet Mahajan. 1986. "Gender Differences in Policy Preferences: A Summary of Trends from the 1960s to the 1980s." *Public Opinion Quarterly* 50:42–61.

Shepsle, Kenneth, and Barry Weingast. 1987. "The Institutional Foundations of Committee Power." *American Political Science Review* 81:85–104.

Sinclair, Barbara. 1995. *Legislators, Leaders, and Lawmaking: The U.S. House of Representatives in the Postreform Era.* Baltimore: Johns Hopkins University Press.

Skocpol, Theda. 1992. *Protecting Soldiers and Mothers: The Political Origins of Social Policy in the United States.* Cambridge, Mass.: Harvard University Press.

———. 1997. *Boomerang: Health Care Reform and the Turn against Government.* New York: W. W. Norton & Co.

Smith, Steven S. 1989. *Call to Order: Floor Politics in the House and Senate.* Washington, D.C.: Brookings Institution.

Smith, Steven S., and Christopher J. Deering. 1990. *Committees in Congress.* 2d ed. Washington, D.C.: Congressional Quarterly.

Stetson, Dorothy McBride. 1997. *Women's Rights in the U.S.A.: Policy Debates and Gender Roles.* 2d ed. New York: Garland Publishing, Inc.

Storing, Herbert J. 1981. *The Anti-Federalist: Writings by Opponents of the Constitution.* Chicago: University of Chicago Press.

Sundquist, James L. 1983. *Dynamics of the Party System: Alignment and Realignment of Political Parties in the United States.* Rev. ed. Washington, D.C.: Brookings Institution.

Swain, Carol M. 1993. *Black Faces, Black Interests: The Representation of African-Americans in Congress.* Cambridge, Mass.: Harvard University Press.

Swers, Michele L. 1998. "Are Congresswomen More Likely to Vote for Women's Issue Bills Than Their Male Colleagues?" *Legislative Studies Quarterly* 23:435–48.

———. 2002. "Transforming the Agenda? Analyzing Gender Differences in Women's Issue Bill Sponsorship." In *Women Transforming Congress,* edited by Cindy Simon Rosenthal. Norman: University of Oklahoma Press, in press.

Tamerius, Karin L. 1995. "Sex, Gender, and Leadership in the Representation of Women." In *Gender Power, Leadership, and Governance,* edited by Georgia Duerst-Lahti and Rita Mae Kelly. Ann Arbor: University of Michigan Press.

Tatalovich, Raymond, and David Schier. 1993. "The Persistence of Ideological Cleavage in Voting on Abortion Legislation in the House of Representatives, 1973–1988." *American Politics Quarterly* 21:125–39.

Thomas, Sue. 1994. *How Women Legislate.* New York: Oxford University Press.

———. 1997. "Why Gender Matters: The Perceptions of Women Officeholders." *Women and Politics* 17:27–53.

Tin, Annie, and Juliana Greenwald. 1995. "'Contract with Family' Welcomed Cautiously by House GOP." *Congressional Quarterly Weekly Report,* 20 May, 1448–50.

Tomz, Michael, Jason Wittenberg, and Gary King. 2001. *Clarify: Software for Interpreting Statistical Results.* Version 2.0. http://gking.harvard.edu/stats.shtml.

Tong, Rosemarie Putnam. 1998. *Feminist Thought: A More Comprehensive Introduction.* 2d ed. Boulder, Colo.: Westview Press.

U.S. Bureau of the Census. 1993. *1990 Census of Population and Housing: Congressional Districts of the United States, 103rd Congress.* Washington, D.C.: U.S. Department of Commerce, Economics and Statistics Administration.

———. 1995. *1990 Census of Population and Housing: Congressional Districts of the United States, 104th Congress.* Washington, D.C.: U.S. Department of Commerce, Economics and Statistics Administration.

Vega, Arturo, and Juanita M. Firestone. 1995. "The Effects of Gender on Congressional Behavior and the Substantive Representation of Women." *Legislative Studies Quarterly* 20:213–22.

Waldman, Steven. 1995. *The Bill: How Legislation Really Becomes Law: A Case Study of the National Service Bill.* New York: Penguin Books.

Weingast, Barry, and William Marshall. 1988. "The Industrial Organization of Congress." *Journal of Political Economy* 91:132–63.

Welch, Susan. 1985. "Are Women More Liberal Than Men in the U.S. Congress?" *Legislative Studies Quarterly* 10:125–34.

Wells, Rob. 1998. "GOP Targets Tax Messages to Women." *Associated Press,* 13 February.

Wilcox, Clyde. 1994. "Why Was 1992 the 'Year of the Woman?' Explaining Women's Gains in 1992." In *The Year of the Woman: Myths and Realities,* edited by Elizabeth Adel Cook, Sue Thomas, and Clyde Wilcox. Boulder, Colo.: Westview Press.

Wilcox, Clyde, and Aage Clausen. 1991. "The Dimensionality of Roll-Call Voting Reconsidered." *Legislative Studies Quarterly* 16:393–406.

Wilson, Rick K., and Cheryl D. Young. 1997. "Cosponsorship in the U.S. Congress." *Legislative Studies Quarterly* 22:25–53.

Wolbrecht, Christina. 2000. *The Politics of Women's Rights: Parties, Positions, and Change.* Princeton, N.J.: Princeton University Press.

———. 2002. "Female Legislators and the Women's Rights Agenda." In *Women Transforming Congress,* edited by Cindy Simon Rosenthal. Norman: University of Oklahoma Press, in press.

Women's Policy, Inc. 1996. *Special Report: First Session of the 104th Congress.* Washington, D.C.: Women's Policy, Inc.

CPSIA information can be obtained
at www.ICGtesting.com
Printed in the USA
LVOW11s2351061116
511882LV00001B/44/P